"I've a grand memory for forgetting."

Robert Louis Stevenson

Expand Your Memory

TIME
LIFE
BOOKS

Other Publications:
WEIGHT WATCHERS® SMART CHOICE RECIPE COLLECTION
THE AMERICAN INDIANS
LOST CIVILIZATIONS
CREATIVE EVERYDAY COOKING
THE ART OF WOODWORKING
TIME-LIFE LIBRARY OF CURIOUS AND UNUSUAL FACTS
HEALTHY HOME COOKING
HOME REPAIR AND IMPROVEMENT
ECHOES OF GLORY
AMERICAN COUNTRY
VOYAGE THROUGH THE UNIVERSE
MYSTERIES OF THE UNKNOWN
UNDERSTANDING COMPUTERS
FIX IT YOURSELF
COUNTRY LIFESTYLES
THE CIVIL WAR
THE ENCHANTED WORLD
TIME FRAME
WINGS OF WAR

For information on and a full description of any of the
Time-Life Books series listed above, please call
1-800-621-7026 weekdays between 9:00 a.m. and 6:00 p.m.
Eastern Standard Time, or write:
Reader Information
Time-Life Customer Service
P.O. Box C-32068
Richmond, Virginia 23261-2068

MINDPOWER

Expand Your Memory

TIME-LIFE BOOKS
Alexandria, Virginia

MINDPOWER

Created, edited, and designed by DK Direct Limited,
23-24 Henrietta Street, London WC2E 8NA

A DORLING KINDERSLEY BOOK

Copyright © 1993 Dorling Kindersley

DK DIRECT LIMITED

Series Editor Reg Grant
Deputy Series Editor Francis Ritter
Editors Karen Bessant, Eleanor Butcher
Editorial Research Nance Fyson

Series Art Editor Ruth Shane
Volume Art Editor Karin Murray
Designers Sean Edwards, Francis Cawley
Picture Research Julia Tacey

Editorial Director Jonathan Reed; **Design Director** Ed Day
Production Manager Ian Paton

Series Consultant Dr. Glenn Wilson
Volume Consultant Dr. Robert Solso
Contributors Professor Mark Ashcraft, Professor John Benjafield,
Dr. Thomas Harrington, Brian Innes, Dr. Alan Pickering

TIME-LIFE BOOKS

President John Hall
Editor-in-Chief Thomas H. Flaherty
Director of Editorial Resources Elise D. Ritter-Clough
Executive Art Director Ellen Robling

Editorial Director Lee Hassig
Marketing Director Regina Hall
Director of Production Services Robert N. Carr
Production Manager Marline Zack

Time-Life Books staff for Expand Your Memory

Editorial Director Robert Doyle
Associate Editor/Research Daniel Kulpinski
Series Consultant Dr. Richard Restak

Time-Life Books is a division of Time-Life Inc.,
a wholly owned subsidiary of THE TIME INC. BOOK COMPANY

Library of Congress Cataloging in Publication Data

Expand your memory
      p.   cm. — (Mindpower ; v. 1)
      "A Dorling Kindersley book" — T.p. verso.
      Includes bibliographical references and index.
      ISBN 0-7835-1254-6 : $14.99
      1. Self-actualization (Psychology) 2. Self-perception. I. Time
-Life Books.   II. Series.
BF637.S4.A77   1993
153.9'3—dc20   92-37435

Printed in United States of America

CONTENTS

INTRODUCTION 6

CHAPTER 1: HOW MEMORY WORKS
TEST YOUR MEMORY 14
UNDERSTAND YOUR MEMORY 18
WORKING MEMORY....................26
MEMORY AND MEANING 30
SCRIPTS AND SCENARIOS 36
VISUAL MEMORY 40
THE POWER OF CONTEXT 48
REMEMBER YOURSELF 52

CHAPTER 2: MEMORY TRICKS
WORKING MNEMONICS 60
VISUAL IMAGERY 66
MEMORY PLACES 74
REMEMBERING FACES 80
REMEMBERING NAMES 84
A HEAD FOR FIGURES 92

CHAPTER 3: OVERCOME FORGETTING
WHY DO WE FORGET? 102
DO YOU REALLY REMEMBER?...........112

CHAPTER 4: BUILD UP YOUR TECHNIQUES
USE WHAT YOU HAVE LEARNED 122
BETTER EVERY DAY 130

SOLUTIONS 136
INDEX 142

INTRODUCTION

MOST PEOPLE CAN EASILY cite instances when their memory has let them down—when a friend's birthday or a colleague's name has been forgotten. Indeed, surveys have shown that about 25 percent of us feel we have a bad memory.

But even a bad memory manages to hold an astonishing amount of information, including the meanings of many thousands of words, ways to perform many different physical tasks, and innumerable details about people and events. American neurologist Richard M. Restak says that just to tick off the number of items your mind is able to hold, you would need to write a zero a second for 90 years. The information your brain contains would fill an encyclopedia 10 billion pages long. With its astounding capacity, your memory acts as a link between the past, present, and future, allowing you to maintain your identity as you update your ideas, skills, and plans in a constantly changing world.

Outstanding memories

Although all of us are born with a huge capacity for remembering information, only a few people seem to make full use of it. A contemporary example of an individual with an extraordinary memory is provided by Englishman Dominic O'Brien, winner of the 1991 World Memory Championships. O'Brien is able to memorize the exact order of 1,820 playing cards (35 packs) and holds the speed record for memorizing one pack—55 seconds. For his own amusement, he has learned all 6,000 questions and answers from the board game Trivial Pursuit. To keep his memory in good working order he memorizes 1,000 randomly generated numbers every day.

To memorize the order of playing cards, or any list of unrelated items, O'Brien employs a memory technique called the method of the loci (see pages 74 to 79). Using this method, he gives each playing card a character—the two of diamonds, for example, is a very tall person—and mentally places them at different locations along a route he knows well. His first route was a local golf course: With three distinct landmarks at each of the 18 holes, he found he could use the golf course to remember up to 54 items, enough for a pack of cards.

One of the best-documented cases of extraordinary memory from the past is that of a Russian reporter, Solomon V. Shereshevskii, often referred to as "S" by psychologists. Studies in the 1920s showed that he could memorize long lists of words and numbers—even nonsense material—and recall them days, months, even years, later. For example, he could remember a table of 400 numbers arranged randomly in a 20-by-20 grid pattern 30 years after having memorized it.

S used standard mnemonic devices of the kind explained in the second chapter of this book (pages 58 to 99). But he also experienced an extreme form of synesthesia, the phenomenon in which information from one sense evokes a memory in another sense (see "A nose for the past" on page 50). A smell might evoke a visual memory, or a conversation he had heard. This synesthesia was important to S's recall because it provided a broader context for everything he remembered.

Infinite storage

Despite his ability to remember virtually everything he saw, heard, or read, S's memory never filled up. Theoretically, there is no limit to the amount of information the memory can store. In fact, the capacity to learn is enhanced by the amount already stored. Stored facts provide a framework on which to build new information.

While the memory's storage capacity is remarkable, scientists estimate that most people tend to remember only about one percent of the information they receive. The brain sifts through the material it receives and stores the key points. This is a crucial mechanism. Although S had a superb memory and almost perfect recall, he did not do well in school. If someone said the same thing to him in two different voices, he recorded the two statements as two separate messages. If someone coughed while S was reading, he remembered the sound as part of the story. His problem was that he

---

Memory search
Each person's memory contains a unique combination of information that is stored in many different ways, and can be accessed from many different *angles. The key to having a good memory is to impose your own logic at the filing stage, so that related items can be pulled out as quickly as possible.*

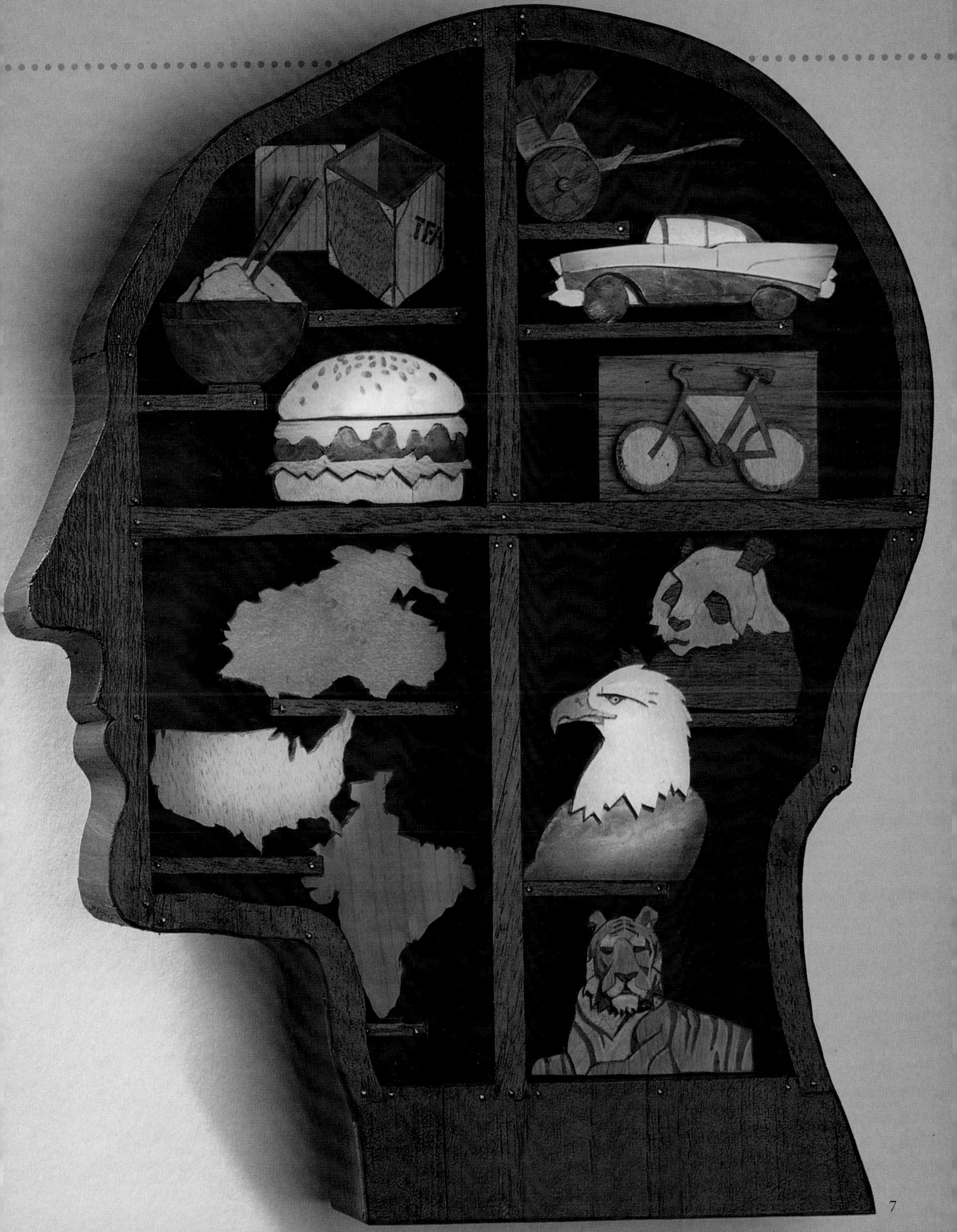

Oral history

Writer Alex Haley traced his ancestors' lives, going back seven generations. His family history was kept in each member's memory, to be passed on orally to the next generation. By listening to this recited history, Haley was able to learn about his ancestry; he chronicled the facts in his book Roots: The Saga of An American Family.

could not forget. His brain did not sift out the unimportant facts, he simply stored everything exactly as he heard it. For S, unpleasant memories never faded away in time.

Although the ability to forget peripheral material is an important part of memory function, most of us would prefer to forget less. To combat the natural tendency to forget, you probably use such devices as writing in a diary or pinning messages on a bulletin board. These techniques serve as adequate practical reminders but are not ideal—what happens when you forget your diary?

Stories from ancestors

In times when ordinary people did not know how to read or write, they had to use their memories more than people do now. Information was passed from generation to generation mainly by stories told and remembered. Constant rehearsal of these stories—in the form of songs and tales—helped to ensure that they would not be lost. Alex Haley, the author of *Roots*, gained vital clues to tracing his own West African origins from details about his slave ancestors related faithfully from generation to generation. These stories were rich in imagery, which enhanced their memorability.

By writing things down instead of making the effort to memorize them, you are merely letting your memory skills deteriorate. Take, for instance, the ability to perform mental arithmetic. Because of the availability of calculators, many people now

TRUE OR FALSE?

Most of us have a general understanding of what memory means. But how much do you really know about memory? Find out by completing the following test. Read through the statements below and mark them true or false. Then turn to page 136 to find out the truth.

1. Memory has a limited storage capacity.................❏

2. Your memory for facts gets worse as you get older.................❏

3. It is harder to remember things that do not interest you..❏

4. Fear increases the ability to remember.❏

5. You can't improve memory.................❏

6. Someone with amnesia has no memory.................❏

7. Getting physical exercise improves memory.................❏

8. What you eat or drink can affect your memory.................❏

9. A vivid memory is an accurate memory.................❏

10. It is easier to learn when you are young.................❏

11. A memory lasts forever.................❏

12. Memories change with time....❏

How Good Is Your Memory?

Many people suspect that their memory is bad, but have no idea whether or not this is really true. It is often difficult to assess how good or bad your memory actually is. Everyone forgets things once in a while and you can never be sure whether you forget more or less than other people.

The following questionnaire will give you a reasonable idea of how well your memory works. For each question, decide which of the options—"never," "rarely," or "often"—represents most accurately the way you have behaved in the past year. Even if some questions do not seem to apply directly to you, try to give each question the most suitable answer. Write your answers down.

1. Do you forget to watch an important television program you intended to watch?

2. Do you forget whether you've turned off a light or heater?

3. Do people's names slip your memory?

4. When you are talking to someone, do you lose the drift of the conversation, perhaps asking: "What were we talking about?"

5. Do you mix and confuse the details of what someone has just told you?

6. Do you find yourself saying "I don't remember that" in conversation?

7. Do you forget to pass on important messages?

8. Do you forget what you went to the store to buy?

9. Do you forget appointments?

10. Do you forget where you have put things—for example, a book—in your house?

11. Do you throw away the thing you want (like the matchbox) and keep what you meant to throw away (the used match)?

12. Do you leave things behind and have to go back and get them?

13. Do you find you can't quite recall a word, although it is on "the tip of your tongue?"

14. Do you have trouble picking up a new skill, even after you have practiced it once or twice?

15. Do you attempt to repeat routine actions —like brushing your hair—when you have just done them?

Now, score your answers. Each "never" counts as 0, "rarely" as 2, and "often" as 4. Add up your score and check it against the categories below.

0-20 points. You scored above average, which reveals that your memory is excellent and effective in a wide range of situations. You seem to experience few memory lapses, and probably have an organized and well-structured lifestyle. Although your memory works very well, you can still improve it. With the help of this volume you will be able to fulfill your true potential.

21-40 points. Your memory is about average. Although you may not be totally satisfied, your memory is basically sound and stable. There may be occasional lapses and mistakes, but nothing that really interferes with your performance or lessens your capabilities. Many of your memory lapses may be due to a lack of concentration. To improve your memory, you should make good use of the memory tricks discussed on pages 58 to 99.

41-60 points. Your memory is below average, but don't be alarmed. You may simply experience more memory lapses because you lead a very busy life. The more there is to remember in a day, the more likely you are to forget some things. You can improve your memory with mental exercise and the use of techniques outlined in this book (see "Memory tricks" on pages 58 to 99). You may also find it useful to structure your activities—to establish routines and keep diaries and notebooks—so that fewer demands are placed on your memory while you are building up your skills.

NUMBER POWER

36552124313028

Can you remember this number? Study it for a few moments, then look away and try to write it down. You will probably find that you can only remember the first two or three digits, and possibly the last few also.

Now break the number down into meaningful chunks: There are 365 days, 52 weeks, and 12 months in a year; approximately 4 weeks in a month; and a month lasts 31, 30, or 28 days. Looking at the number in this new way, try to memorize it again. You will almost certainly find that you remember it accurately.

This technique is also discussed in the "A head for figures" section on pages 92 to 99.

forget some information. The third chapter of the book looks at why memories are sometimes forgotten or distorted, along with ways to guard against such loss. A final chapter puts all the memory techniques together for everyday use.

While no one can work magic overnight by using the methods described in this volume, you can definitely improve your memory to some degree. With practice, the techniques will become familiar and you will be able to memorize and recall information with greater speed and accuracy.

Polishing up your skills
With the passage of time, memories can become dull and unclear, but with a little effort you can easily polish them up.

Techniques exist that will allow you to remember facts, events, names, numbers, and faces with greater clarity and accuracy.

have great difficulty doing even relatively simple sums in their heads. Practice could remedy this situation. You need to exercise your memory so you can use it effectively when the need arises.

Improving memory

To be able to use your memory to its full potential, you need to understand it. The first chapter of this volume discusses the logical and structured way in which memory works. Following this is a chapter that teaches you how to maximize your memory potential through a variety of techniques. These strategies will help you memorize a wide range of material more effectively—telephone numbers, names, birthdays, grocery lists. Once you know the basic techniques, remembering anything will become much easier. The key to success is making the effort to apply the techniques.

No matter what techniques you use, you will still

BREAK THE CODE

Imagine you are a spy. You have to memorize the following coded message as quickly as possible.

E S H S A
S R K I W T C

Could you do this? At first glance, such an arbitrary arrangement of letters seems very difficult to remember accurately. There is, however, a hidden pattern in the coded message that, once recognized, will make the letters instantly memorable. Before you read any further, spend approximately one minute seeing if you can spot the hidden pattern.

The secret is this: Working backwards from the bottom right-hand corner, the letters spell the words "cats whiskers." Once you know this, you can easily remember the message and re-create the arrangement of the letters. This trick demonstrates one of the basic principles of memory improvement: Organizing random material into a meaningful form always makes it easier to remember.

CHAPTER ONE

HOW MEMORY WORKS

WITHOUT A MEMORY you could not reason, communicate, or plan for the future. Despite the importance of this mental function, however, you probably only think about memory when it has let you down or when it springs inexplicably into action—when an incident you observe or a snatch of overheard conversation suddenly conjures up a vivid recollection, for example.

For years scientists have been trying to unravel the workings of memory. Studies have established that it is not a single system but one that has many components that together store bits of knowledge for various lengths of time, from a few seconds to a lifetime. Different parts of your memory store different kinds of information, everything from visual images to fascinating facts, childhood memories, and knowledge of acquired skills, like riding a bike.

Your memory does not occupy one definable area but is distributed throughout the outer layers of the brain. Billions of nerve cells, called neurons, make up these layers. Each neuron is connected to thousands of others. As you learn, your mind encodes each memory into these neural networks; the neurons then branch out to form new circuits by making additional connections with other neurons. When you recall a memory, a particular set of neurons jumps into action.

Problems in this complex system can have strange effects. If, for example, you had a defect in your visual memory you would not be able to recognize a familiar face or object. One man even mistook his wife for a hat because of such a defect. He regularly misidentified everyday objects and could only recognize familiar people by their voices. In all other respects his memory was intact; he was in fact a successful music teacher.

Understanding how your memory works, you are more likely to be able to use it to full advantage. For example, by knowing that a particular environment can activate a dormant memory, you will realize that the way to recover forgotten events is to go back to the places where events transpired. This chapter examines the complex workings of memory from a practical standpoint. Armed with a better understanding, you will be able to improve the speed with which you store and recall information in the future.

YOUR BRAIN STORES MEMORIES IN A LOGICAL WAY,
LINKING RELATED MEMORIES TOGETHER, SO YOU CAN
RECALL THEM MORE EASILY.

TEST YOUR MEMORY

YOUR MEMORY CAN STORE vast quantities of disparate information—everything from your friends' birthdays to the dates of the Punic Wars—to be recalled at will even years later. But sometimes memories can be recalled only for a short period. For example, it is difficult to remember where you parked the car in the city last weekend although you had no trouble finding it at the time.

The exercises on the following pages should give you some insight into why it is that you can remember certain things while forgetting most others. After completing each of the exercises, read the pertinent section of "Your memory in action" on page 17, which will explain your results.

1. How long is your memory span?

Test your short-term memory on the following sequences of numbers:

2
71
692
4217
71821
594317
3718656
59184674
795847659
3948598286
97385382958

Ask a friend to read the numbers to you, digit by digit, one line at a time. After each line has been read to you, repeat it aloud. Your friend should then move on to the next string of numbers. Continue in this fashion until you encounter a line that you are unable to repeat correctly from memory. The number of digits in the last line that you successfully parrot is your memory's digit span. This is the limit on the number of digits that you can hold at once in your short-term memory. To find out how your short-term memory for digits compares with that of other people, turn to page 17.

2. What's your name and what do you do?

Have a look at the people on these two pages. Spend about two minutes studying their faces, names, and occupations. Then test your memory by turning to the box on page 16.

MS. HAMMEL
PAINTER

MS. GRANT
PILOT

MR. LENNARD
PLUMBER

DR. SCHMIDT
PHILOSOPHER

MR. VAN DEN BROEK
ENTREPRENEUR

MS. CARROL
SECRETARY

MR. THATCHER
ELECTRICIAN

MR. CLAYMAN
ENGINEER

MRS. WHITE
SALES PERSON

MRS. TACEY
VIOLINIST

MRS. JACKSON
AIR HOSTESS

MISS. MEDIN
TEACHER

MR. MACDUFF
JOURNALIST

MR. CLARK
TRANSLATOR

MR. PLOTNIK
ART DEALER

3. Random effects

Study the objects below for five seconds. Then close the book and write down all the objects that you can remember. After checking to see how many you got right, turn to page 17.

What's your name again?

These are the same faces you saw on pages 14 and 15, but their names and occupations are missing. On a piece of paper, write down all of the names and occupations that you can recall, then check them against pages 14 and 15 to see how many you got right. Did you remember more names or more occupations? To find out what this tells you about your memory, see the "Your memory in action" box opposite.

4. List recall

Read through the following list of words, just once. Then, close the book and write down all the words that you can remember. After you have checked to see how many words you remembered correctly, consult "Your memory in action," opposite.

5. Visual memories

Look at the following images for a few seconds, then close the book. Wait five minutes and write down what you can remember. Check your answers and proceed to "Your memory in action" opposite.

canoe	sawbuck	nostril
which	case	lumber
cat	white	clearly
fee	left	superhero
stair	sailor	coffee
subway	church	age
inch	together	light
grass	steel	skill

YOUR MEMORY IN ACTION

1. The number of digits you remembered reveals how many individual items you can hold in your short-term memory at one time. Most people can recall between five and seven digits; recalling fewer than four digits is below average, and remembering eight or more digits is exceptional. Seven is a common limit for short-term memory.

2. Because occupations bring a picture to mind while names are purely abstract, people who take this test usually recall about twice as many occupations as names. Since your brain stores names and faces in different places, you may sometimes have a vivid memory for the face while having no idea of the name that goes with it. For tips on improving your performance see "Remembering names" on pages 84 to 91.

3. When presented with random information, your mind immediately tries to make sense of what it sees. Six of these 11 random items are birds. Because your mind automatically groups them into a single category, you will probably have remembered these items best. Truly random information is almost impossible to remember, but any sort of pattern can make the mental work much easier.

4. You probably remembered more words from the beginning and end of the list than you did from the middle. This is an example of an effect called the "serial position phenomenon." What happened was that you paid particular attention to the first few words, thus causing them to be stored in long-term memory; words at the end of the list, on the other hand, benefited from being the most recent entries in your short-term memory. You may have recalled fewer items on this test than you did on the previous one. This was because there was no obvious category—like birds—to which the words could be assigned.

5. The image you are least likely to have forgotten is that of the soccer player kicking bananas. According to the "von Restorff effect," named for the German psychologist who first demonstrated it, you remember best things that are unexpected. Since soccer players do not normally kick bananas, the image probably planted itself firmly in your mind.

UNDERSTAND YOUR MEMORY

MEMORY IS BOTH fascinating and frustrating—and in nearly equal measures. Sometimes it performs with seemingly effortless brilliance at unexpected moments, and yet it routinely fails in the most mundane and familiar situations.

The complex and unpredictable way memory functions has fascinated philosophers, scientists, and psychologists, for hundreds of years. Their studies have produced a model of how memory works that answers many of the questions associated with remembering, even if some of the problems still remain unsolved.

Today, psychologists agree that memory can be seen not as a single unified entity, but as a system with three parts that are constantly interacting with one another. The three parts of the system are known as sensory memory, short-term memory, and long-term memory. They all work together, sending pieces of information to and from each other, and each has a definable function and a measurable length.

How long is short?

Most people think short-term memory is responsible for holding recent memories, from perhaps an hour or a day ago. This is not so. Scientists describe short-term memory as the system that holds something—a telephone number, for example, or a sentence—in your mind during the period of time it takes you to make sense of it. The length of short-term memory is about 30 seconds at most. Anything that you remember for longer, from a few minutes to 70 years, is in long-term memory. So if you forget to telephone a friend or run an errand, it is not your short-term memory that is letting you down but your long-term memory.

Most memory lapses, from failing to remember a new colleague's name to forgetting the height of Mount Everest, result from a failure to retrieve information from long-term memory. Yet ironically, the data stored in long-term memory is there for a lifetime, encoded in the neural pathways of the brain. It can, however, be difficult to access because the storehouse of memories is so vast.

The third type of memory capacity is called sensory memory. Sensory memories (primarily storing sights and sounds) are the most short-lived of the three types, lasting a fleeting four seconds at most.

Memory like a sieve

The short-term memory makes sense of the input the brain receives from the outside world. It acts like a sieve, sorting out what will be preserved and what will be allowed to fall into oblivion. Any effort to remember the information that enters the short-term memory ensures that it is passed on to the long-term memory for permanent storage. Otherwise, it will be forgotten in just 15 to 30 seconds. As the 18th-century English writer Samuel Johnson wisely observed, "The true art of memory is the art of attention."

The most striking aspects of short-term memory are just how short and fragile it is. The only way you can extend it beyond 30 seconds is by what psychologists call rehearsal—repeating the information in your head. Imagine you are using a pay phone. There is heavy traffic noise all around. You phone the operator to get the number of an acquaintance. As she gives you the number, you realize you do not have a pen to write it down. You know that if you do not keep repeating the number, you will not remember it long enough to be able to find a pen. You also know that if you stop reciting the number and ask someone to lend you a pen, the number will slip through your memory. It is a bit like juggling 10 oranges in the air: You must concentrate hard, and the slightest interference—speaking to someone, hearing a loud noise, or even looking at a cat walking by—and those oranges will suddenly be at your feet again.

Filed away

Visualize long-term memory as a filing cabinet stuffed full of images. Your memory decides where to store information, using a logical system. The system is very flexible, however. It enables you to bring an image to mind from a variety of different starting points in the cabinet.

WHEN SHORT BECOMES LONG

To understand the difference between short- and long-term memory, read the following set of letters just once. Read them out loud at a steady pace. The moment you have finished reading them, look away and say them back again:

s d j c u w f

You may well have been able to recite all or most of the letters correctly. Now read them again, and then immediately look away and start counting backward in threes from 486—486, 483, 480, 477, and so on, as quickly as you can—stopping when you get to 429.

Now see if you can remember the string of letters. You probably cannot remember them. The reason is that you were not allowed to rehearse them; your mind was busy concentrating on the mental arithmetic. This arithmetic took time—approximately 30 seconds, the outer limit of your short-term memory. So if you did remember any of the letters, you probably had already transferred them into your long-term memory.

The next main type of memory is long-term memory. Long-term memory is equally responsible for information taken in 10 years ago and facts learned in just the past few minutes. But different aspects of long-term memory appear to handle different sorts of information.

For example, one area is concerned with personal details, those memories that will be unique to each person: What you ate for lunch, your spouse's name, and what you did during summer vacation, for example. Another area processes general knowledge, such as the chemical formula for sulfuric acid, the date of the first moon landing, or the distance between New York and San Francisco. There is also the sort of long-term memory that keeps track of motor skills such as how to drive, type, or play an instrument.

Fleeting impressions

The third type of memory, and the most fleeting, is sensory memory. It is the first gathering point for any information entering your brain through your senses. Sensory memory gathers and momentarily holds stimuli from the outside world: Sights, sounds, smells, tastes, and the feel of things. If you imagine short- and long-term memory as chambers in which ideas are stored temporarily or permanently, then sensory memory would be the corridor outside the chambers. The corridor is full of the sights, sounds, and smells encountered every second of every day. If all those sights and sounds

Learning lines
An actor playing the part of Shakespeare's Hamlet must commit to memory 1,539 lines of speech. To achieve this extraordinary feat he rehearses them in his 30-second short-term memory until they are permanently imprinted on his durable long-term memory. During a performance of the play, other actors' lines will act as cues for him to recall his own responses from long-term storage.

MEMORY DECEIVES THE EYE

The way the three memory systems constantly connect with and influence one another is evident whenever you read material that seems familiar. Undemanding magazines, newspapers, and comic strips are good examples of this type of material. Because you rely on the knowledge stored in your long-term memory, you don't pay as close attention to the printed words as you might if you were reading more difficult material, such as a textbook. Sometimes the familiarity is so strong that you will miss typograpical errors or just not see what is there. Read this sentence:

FINISHED FILES ARE THE
RESULT OF YEARS OF SCIENTIFIC
STUDY COMBINED WITH THE
EXPERIENCE OF MANY YEARS

Now go back and read it again, counting the Fs. If you counted fewer than six, you should count again. It is hard to find all of them because three of them occur in the word "of," a word we tend to skip over in sensory processing because of its relative lack of meaning. (Incidentally, did you also spot the mistake in the word "typographical," 12 lines above?)

Careful reading
If you read "Paris in the Spring" on the sign, try reading it again. People read this sign incorrectly because their long-term memory dredges up the familiar phrase in response to the stimulus of the sign—and also informs them that the word "the" is unlikely to occur twice in a row.

could enter the chamber, chaos would result. But they cannot. There are doors between the corridor and the chambers, blocking the flow so that only some of the information can pass through.

Wherever you are and whatever you are doing, your senses are being bombarded with information. Most of this information stays in the corridor for two to four seconds, where you are unaware of it. If you are reading a book, for example, and the radio is on in the same room, you will not hear what is on the radio as long as your attention is on the book. The sound lingers for a few moments in the corridor and then is gone. But if something attracts your attention to the radio, a door opens to your short-term or long-term memory, and you become conscious of the sound.

Working together

The three memory systems continually interact in most everyday situations. The act of watching television, for example, uses all the components of memory. Imagine the following situation: Mary is watching a cooking program, following the recipe

for making chocolate mousse. The television chef says, "Separate the yolks from the whites—but make sure they are at room temperature."

Mary's sensory memory picks up the sounds from the television. She retrieves words and word meanings from her long-term memory, and places them in her short-term memory so she can understand the meaning of the sentence she is hearing.

Mary is retrieving other information from long-term memory at the same time. When she hears "make sure they are at room temperature" she thinks to herself, "the eggs are in the refrigerator, and it will take them at least half an hour to warm up." Mary has accessed many kinds of general knowledge stored in her long-term memory in order to make this calculation.

While Mary was thinking this, she missed what the chef was saying next, except for the last few seconds of his speech, when he said, "because they were still cold." This remains in her auditory sensory memory; the rest of what the chef said is long gone from the sensory register, which, as we have seen, holds input for only a few seconds. Mary

MEMORY ON THE MOVE

Which memory functions are called into play when you walk down the road, recognize, and greet a friend? The answer is, all of them. Here is what happens in that situation: As Bob walks down the street, information about his surroundings is held briefly in his sensory memory. Unless he focuses on any of the stimuli by attending to them in his short-term memory, all input will slip from his sensory memory in a matter of seconds.

As someone walks toward him, however, he takes notice. His sensory memory takes in the image of the approaching person's face and refers it to his long-term memory to retrieve information about her. This information, such as her name and how he knows her, is forwarded to Bob's short-term memory, which tries to make sense of these suggestions but finds an apparent contradiction.

Bob's stored knowledge of this friend, whose name is Janet, does not match with the fact that the person he sees has curly hair. His sensory memory needs another image, so his eyes scan her face a little more closely for more data. As Janet speaks his name, he realizes that it is indeed his friend. His short-term memory sends the new information to his long-term memory, which needs updating. Next time he will recognize Janet with her new hair style.

Seeing a friend

Even in a simple situation like walking down the road and recognizing a friend, the three memory systems work together to produce a comprehensible view of the world. When Bob sees Janet coming toward him, his long-term memory is accessed for biographical information about her: Who she is and how he comes to know her.

now divides her attention between listening to the rest of the recipe and trying to write it down on a piece of paper. But just at the moment when the chef says how much chocolate to use, the telephone rings. Because there is not enough space in her short-term memory to attend to three different tasks—listening to the chef, writing, and answering the phone, Mary gives up and decides to write the show later for the recipe.

The way the three memory functions interact is clearly illustrated here. Sensory memory continually takes in sights and sounds from the television.

At the same time, Mary retrieves long-term memory knowledge in order to understand the recipe. She holds the new ideas and thoughts in short-term memory and then feeds some of the material back into long-term memory.

Try analyzing an everyday task you perform frequently—reading a book or feeding the cat—in a similar way. Work out which kind of memory is being used at any moment, sensory, short-term, or one of the kinds of long-term. Once you understand the overall patterns of memory, you will be better equipped to use it to best effect.

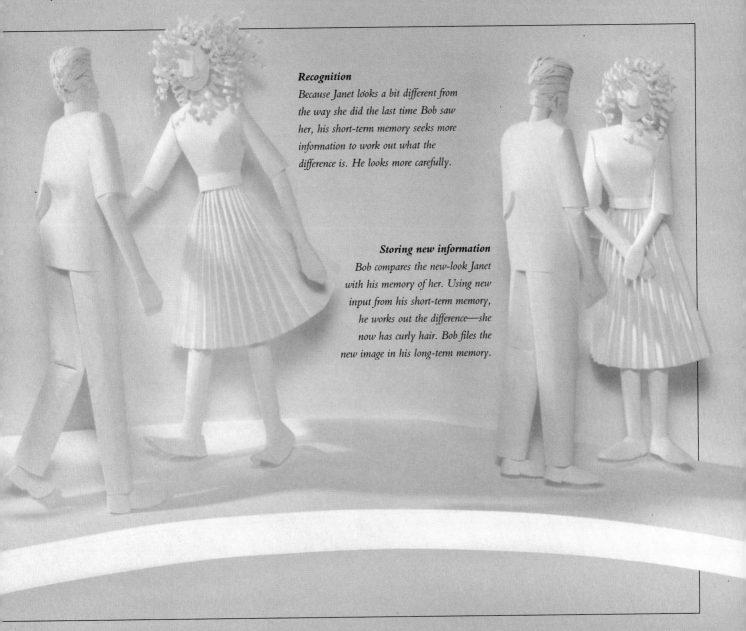

Recognition
Because Janet looks a bit different from the way she did the last time Bob saw her, his short-term memory seeks more information to work out what the difference is. He looks more carefully.

Storing new information
Bob compares the new-look Janet with his memory of her. Using new input from his short-term memory, he works out the difference—she now has curly hair. Bob files the new image in his long-term memory.

SHADOWS OF THOUGHT

One of the most elusive goals of the scientific study of memory has been to discover where memories are located in the neural tissue of the brain—or if, in fact, they have a precise location at all.

In the 1950s, Canadian neurosurgeon Wilder Penfield directly stimulated the surface of patients' brains with electrodes during brain surgery. Only local anesthesia was required for the operations, so the patients were fully conscious. When some areas of their brain surfaces were stimulated, the patients would experience vivid memories or dreamlike episodes from the past. Penfield concluded that the memories of a lifetime are stored in the vast network of nerve cells in the cerebral cortex.

The advent of computer technology has since taken the study of memory and the brain much further. Scientists can for the first time examine the living brains of perfectly healthy people. The latest

MAPPING MEMORY

Recent technological innovations have brought scientists closer to answering the many questions about how memory works. One crucial advance has been the development of the mental activity network scanner (MANSCAN). This device uses electroencephalography (EEG) to record brain activity electronically from 124 points around the skull. It then matches the data with an image of the head produced by a magnetic resonance imaging (MRI) scan. This reveals exactly where in the brain the activity is taking place. By correlating all the data, the MANSCAN is capable of producing pictures of brain activity every four-thousandths of a second. Looked at in succession, pictures chart the bursts of neural activity in the brain as the subject performs different tasks.

By continuing to evaluate brain activity with the precision and sophistication offered by MANSCAN, scientists may be able to work out exactly what structural and functional changes take place in our neural networks during learning and memory functions.

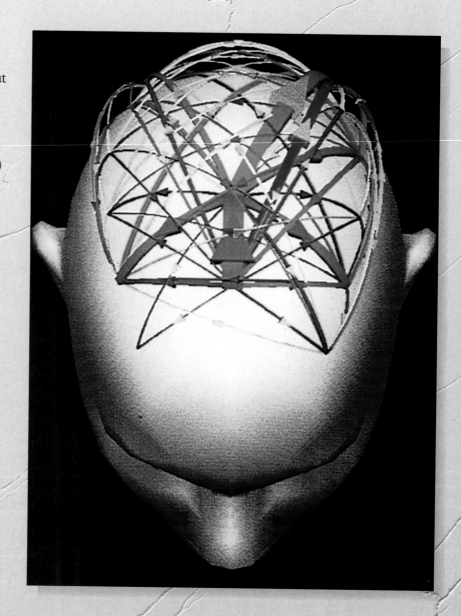

technology allows neurologists to develop pictures of "shadows of thought." By tracing the electrical activity of the brain, it is now possible to observe the path of a thought from point to point.

Scientists are beginning to create precise maps of brain activity that correspond to different acts of remembering. Such maps reveal that for any memory to occur, a complex interaction between many areas of the brain must take place.

PICTURES OF THE FUTURE

Positron emission tomography (PET) scanning provides pictures of brain activity while a subject performs a range of mental tasks: Seeing, hearing, speaking, and thinking. Distinctly different areas of the brain light up to reveal activity as each task is performed. The colors correspond to levels of nerve response: Red areas indicate intense activity, while blue areas mean relatively little brain activity.

Using a combination of PET's superior ability to accurately define areas of activity. and MANSCAN's capacity for tracing the movement of the brain waves (see opposite), scientists predict that they will be able to provide spectacular motion pictures of memory in action by the end of the 20th century.

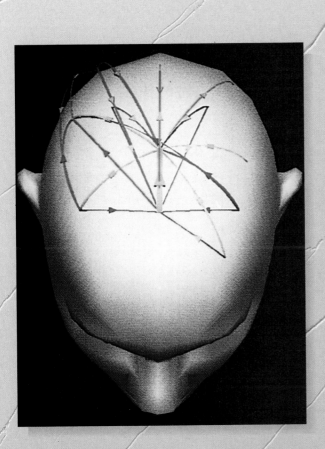

Neural–activity patterns
These two MANSCAN pictures show the difference between a task requiring short-term memory (left) and one that does not (above). Clearly, using short-term memory greatly increases the complexity of the brain activity. This kind of research can be used to predict whether or not a person is about to perform a memory task correctly, spelling hope for the diagnosis of neural disease and the evaluation of new drugs and rehabilitation therapies.

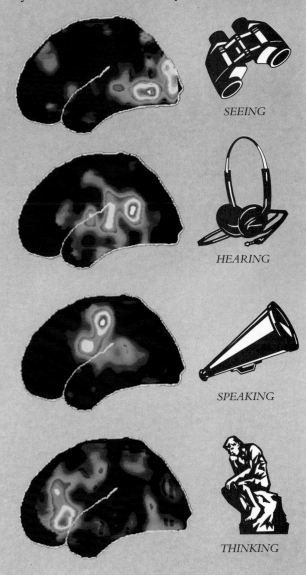

SEEING

HEARING

SPEAKING

THINKING

WORKING MEMORY

WHEN PEOPLE TALK ABOUT improving their memory, it is long-term memory they have in mind. They want to be able to remember names and faces, facts and numbers, for a considerable period of time. But most people don't realize that the ultimate key to improving long-term memory performance lies in the efficiency of the short-term memory system.

Short-term memory is the workshop where material is selected, sorted, and encoded for storage in the permanent vaults of long-term memory. It also plays an important part in retrieving memories from the long-term collection. Because it performs all these functions, short-term memory is often called working memory.

Making sense
The short-term memory has to sift through information constantly to make sense of the world, sorting out a continuous onslaught of stimulation. Some information is allowed through and is retained in long-term memory, while other material is sifted out and forgotten.

The first key to sharpening short-term memory is attention. For example, you will not be able to recall a license plate number from the scene of an accident if you do not focus your full attention on it. Your eyes may physically see the license number, causing it to be held for a split second in your sensory memory, but if the information is not attended to by your short-term memory function and consequently not processed into your long-term memory, you will not be able to recall it.

This type of attention is a form of concentration. So by forcing yourself to concentrate, you can actually force your short-term memory to work better. If you concentrate on what you are seeing and hearing, and thereby allow that information to pass into your short-term memory for processing, there is a good chance that it will be pushed into long-term memory for permanent storage.

You cannot rely on your sensory memory to memorize things. You must apply your short-term memory to the task as well. You will not remember anything about a book you are studying if you are daydreaming about something else at the same time: Your eyes may be fixed on the pages, feeding the words to your visual sensory memory, but unless you concentrate on them and transfer them to your short-term memory, they will soon go.

Know your limits

Like any complex machine, your memory system has limitations. To operate at maximum efficiency, you must first understand these limitations. We know that despite the short-term memory's crucial role in processing information from sensory to long-term memory, its working time is short and its storage capacity is small. This is because in order to act as an efficient sieve or filter, it must be free of any permanent memories itself—the long-term memory is the place for permanent thoughts.

As the first test on page 14 demonstrated, your short-term memory can hold only around seven items at once—seven digits, perhaps, or seven letters. Psychologists call this the "Magic seven" rule. It is as if short-term memory is powered by a battery that has only so much power at any one moment. The battery is strong enough to retain four or five letters in consciousness, but it does not have enough power for 10 letters.

SEEING THINGS

When you see a flash of lightning or the path of light described by a flashlight circling in the dark, you are in fact seeing a memory trace preserved by your visual sensory memory. What you see as a flash of lightning actually consists of three or four successive flashes, each one lasting a thousandth of a second. But your sensory memory holds the image of each flash for a quarter to a half-second, creating the illusion of a continuous flash.

It is also your sensory memory that creates the illusion of continuous movement when you watch a movie. What you are seeing is thousands of separate still pictures interspersed with brief periods of darkness. Your sensory memory stores these individual pictures long enough between frames to allow them to merge and thus create the impression of fluid movement.

The images in a flip book are seen at much farther intervals apart, but they still approximate the same fluidity. This is because your visual sensory memory is longer than the time gap between the still images on the moving pages.

Making a motion picture
By turning the corner of this page backward and forward, you can create the illusion of a man is strumming his guitar. The animation works because your sensory memory holds each image for up to a half-second after it has disappeared from view, so creating a link between one image and the next.

THE MAGIC SEVEN

The average number of units that the short-term memory can hold is seven. But you can still read and remember an unfamiliar sentence such as "Do leave your shoes outside the door," which consists of 30 letters. This is because with the letters grouped into words, each word becomes a single unit: As you can remember seven units, you can remember seven words.

Try an experiment for yourself. Read the following string of letters out loud once, as evenly as you can. Then look away and say them back in the same order: j w h d o c t.

Now read the following words in exactly the same way: hat, can, bee, fox, pit, rye, gem. This test also involves retaining seven items, even though you have to remember 21 letters.

You probably found it no more difficult to remember the string of unrelated words than to remember the unrelated letters. This principle is widely exploited in memory improvement techniques.

By grouping smaller items into larger chunks, you can dramatically reduce the strain imposed on your memory.

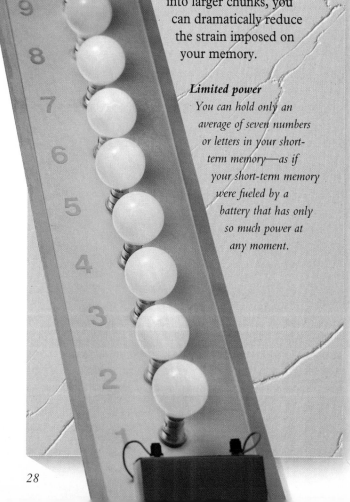

Limited power
You can hold only an average of seven numbers or letters in your short-term memory—as if your short-term memory were fueled by a battery that has only so much power at any moment.

Even this limited memory capacity is threatened by distractions and interruptions. Try this simple test: Read an unfamiliar seven-digit phone number out loud. Then try to write it down, but in the middle of writing it say the word "pet." You will probably find it impossible to do both these things at once. By transferring your attention to speaking that one word, you have exceeded the attention capacity of your short-term memory and pushed out the memory of the phone number.

Value of interference

Most interference comes from sensory memory, which is constantly nudging short-term memory with input about surroundings. But there are also advantages to the fact that attention tends to wander. Imagine how difficult life would be if you weren't able to be distracted. Sitting in an airport lounge reading a newspaper, for instance, you would never hear the announcement of your flight.

Knowing that short-term memory can be so easily thwarted might help you plan work more effectively. You might decide that it is not such a good idea to have the radio on while you are studying an important document. You might also question the wisdom of large, open office work areas with all their inevitable distractions.

Hard to improve

You cannot significantly increase your short-term memory span. If you practiced the digit test on page 14, you might find that you could increase the number of digits you recalled. The improvement, however, would not be in your short-term memory's storage capacity. You would probably have learned to instantly group the digits into units of two or three, but you would still remember only seven units (see box, left).

Similarly, the time you can retain something in your short-term memory cannot be extended beyond the 30-second limit, except by constant rehearsal. If you repeat the information over and over, each time you say it to yourself you restart the 30-second stopwatch. But if you are interrupted in this rehearsal, the information will be displaced and consequently lost.

So, short-term memory is short and easily disturbed, yet it must constantly process an enormous

amount of information. It appears that short–term memory cannot be forced to hold information for longer than 30 seconds, and you cannot overcome its tendency to be easily interrupted. However, its working relationship with long-term memory is something that you really can improve.

If you set out deliberately to memorize a piece of information, it is your short-term memory that you consciously apply to the task. By actively attending to the information and processing it, you try to ensure that it will be stored in a retrievable form. Your short-term memory does this constantly and automatically, but the techniques described in this book will help you to get short-term memory to work even better.

In general, memory techniques help your short-term memory give meaning to items before it puts them in permanent storage, thus providing hooks to help you pull the memories out of storage at a later date. If your short-term memory can learn to organize material for quick and efficient retrieval, you will be able to exploit the vast innate capacity of long-term memory to the fullest.

Short-term memory capacity

Your short-term memory has a limited capacity. You can concentrate on only one thing at a time with any accuracy or speed. This is why you wouldn't be able to hold a conversation, listen to the radio, read a book, and write a letter all at the same time, even if you had four arms!

MEMORY AND MEANING

LONG-TERM MEMORY IS continually storing new information. It can take in an almost infinite amount of knowledge and, except when memory capacity has been reduced because of brain damage, can preserve the material indefinitely. But much of the information in your long-term memory is impossible to recall. For example, can you remember what you were wearing on Wednesday a month ago, or what the weather was like on March 14 last year? You paid attention to these things at the time, so why can't you remember them now? The problem lies in recalling the information—gaining access to it at a later date. To improve your ability to do this, you must first understand how information is stored in your memory. If you know how the memory went in, you will have a better chance of getting it out later.

Organized thoughts

You can retrieve a memory more easily from the vast mental warehouse of information if it has been stored in a logical, orderly way. Imagine how difficult it would be to find a particular book in the library if it were not cataloged. Memories, too, are

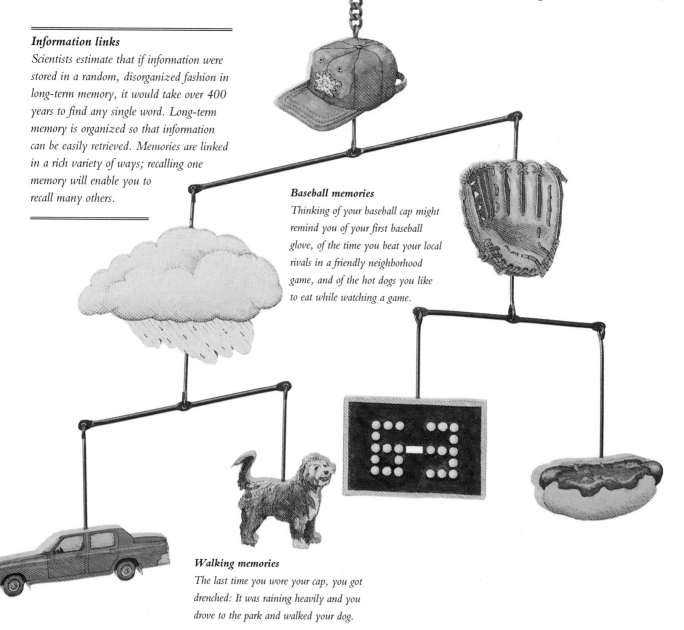

Information links
Scientists estimate that if information were stored in a random, disorganized fashion in long-term memory, it would take over 400 years to find any single word. Long-term memory is organized so that information can be easily retrieved. Memories are linked in a rich variety of ways; recalling one memory will enable you to recall many others.

Baseball memories
Thinking of your baseball cap might remind you of your first baseball glove, of the time you beat your local rivals in a friendly neighborhood game, and of the hot dogs you like to eat while watching a game.

Walking memories
The last time you wore your cap, you got drenched: It was raining heavily and you drove to the park and walked your dog.

Domino effect

When you next have trouble remembering something, try thinking about a related piece of information. One fact or idea often brings others to mind in a domino effect.

cataloged so that related facts and ideas are linked together. You can make use of this order by creating mental links yourself when you store new information—a technique often used in memory tricks. When information is linked, one memory triggers the release of related bits of knowledge.

Information stored in long-term memory falls into three categories: Personal experiences, general knowledge of the world, and "how-to" knowledge. Psychologists refer to these three types of memories as episodic, semantic, and procedural. Together, they contain all the information you have accumulated over a lifetime.

Personal records

Episodic memory is your autobiographical record-keeping system and contains a wealth of personal experience, from the names of your elementary-school teachers to what you had for dinner last night. These memories are unique to you, and just as no one else has your fingerprints, no two people will have the same set of personal memories. Even when a group of people experience the same event, their memories of it will differ. For example, you may remember how slow the service was in a restaurant, but little else about the meal. Your friends, on the other hand, recall not the service but the delicious food and the snowstorm they battled through on the way home.

Episodic memories are linked chronologically. Events that occur together are time-dated, placed in your memory "diary," and linked to other events that occurred at a similar time. For instance, you might recall with certainty that something happened in March because you remember seeing daffodils at the time. This chronological linking principle gives episodic memories a somewhat

I REMEMBER WHEN...

Because the memories of events that occurred near the same time are stored together, the best way to recall a forgotten detail is to cue yourself with other events from that same time in your life.

Suppose that you are trying to remember your fifth-grade teacher's name. When you try to visualize the teacher's face, you think about the school building, your classmates, or the house where you lived. You may recall one particularly memorable incident, such as when you were publicly reprimanded by the teacher for your part in a classroom prank. One clue can lead to another and eventually, by what might seem like a rather random route, you remember your teacher's name.

haphazard quality—facts which just happened to occur at the same time are stored together. This means that events as diverse as passing your driving test and the death of your pet goldfish could be linked in your personal memory bank.

One memory often triggers other related ones. Even years later, hearing a song from your youth will conjure up a whole set of images: Where you were when you heard it, what you were doing, and the friends who were with you. Test this yourself. What was your favorite song in high school? What people and events do you associate with it? Does this conjure up a whole set of related memories?

World knowledge

The second main component of long-term memory, semantic memory, holds your general world knowledge, which breaks down into two major categories. First, there is knowledge of meaning in language—the mental dictionary with its rules for putting ideas into words and weaving words into language. Using this dictionary, you know that the word "happy" is an adjective, and you can identify the emotion it describes. The second category within semantic memory is conceptual knowledge—an encyclopedia of information about concepts, ideas, objects, and the relationships between them. This mental encyclopedia contains not only

MEMORY FOR WORLD EVENTS

Where were you in 1987? You may find this very difficult to answer. But if you are told that 1987 was the year of the Iran-Contra hearings, the Wall Street crash, and the release of the film *Crocodile Dundee*, you will have more chance of coming up with some answers. If these public events, or others like them, had an impact on your personal life, they became encoded in your episodic memory. Because of this you can remember what you were doing at the time.

But facts about world events in 1987 that had little effect on you personally are only stored in your semantic memory. The following test measures your semantic knowledge of world events from 1987. The answers are on page 136.

1. Which Austrian political figure was banned from entering the U.S. because of his role in World War II?
2. What famous Hollywood dancer died in this year?
3. What is the name of the U.S. Navy frigate that was hit by Exocet missiles in the Persian Gulf?
4. Which European prime minister was elected for a third term?
5. What painting was sold at Christies in London for a record £24 million?
6. What infamous war criminal died in Spandau Prison in West Berlin?

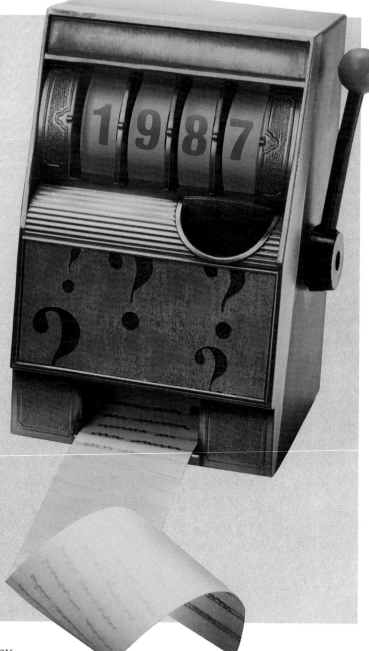

the knowledge that an elephant is a large, gray, four-legged mammal, but also considerable related information, such as the fact that there are two types of elephants, Indian and African, that their diets consist of vegetation, and that they are both hunted illegally for their ivory tusks.

The organizing principle for semantic memory is relatedness—things that are similar in meaning are stored together. For example, your semantic memory contains your familiarity with the word "truck," as well as your knowledge about its concept—what it represents. You know general things about the concept—a truck is used for hauling things. You also know how the word is used: "The truck hit the car" is fine, but "The truck greeted the car" is not. All this information is stored in your semantic memory according to the relatedness

principle. Included in your "truck" concept is your awareness of delivery trucks, dump trucks, and moving vans, plus the knowledge that trucks have engines, brakes, and steering wheels. Some information is central to your "truck" concept; for example, the fact that trucks transport goods is more important than the fact that some of them are red or that they are often dirty. The most important information tends to be recalled first because those retrieval cues are strongest.

Using the general knowledge stored in your semantic memory, you also have the ability to reason and draw inferences. You "know" things that you have never learned directly because you can infer that they are true based on the knowledge stored in your semantic memory. This is how you can answer questions with educated guesses. It is unlikely that you ever learned the answers to the questions: Did Julius Caesar have a mother? Does a kiwi fruit have seeds? But you can infer the answers from general knowledge in your semantic memory about how humans and fruits reproduce.

Semantic memory plays a key role in our comprehension of language. As you read or hear the words in a sentence, related concepts and definitions are activated, or primed, in your memory. Once this has happened, your working, or short-term, memory can retrieve them. This priming effect guides comprehension. For example, when reading the sentence "Bill and Mary saw the mountains as they were flying to California," the words "Bill" and "Mary" (indicating passengers) together with "flying" activate the idea of airplane travel, and the word "mountains" fits what you know about scenery observed through an airplane window. Priming and general knowledge guide you away from implausible interpretations (could the mountains be flying to California?).

Practice makes perfect
The third type of long-term memory, procedural memory, stores the motor skills you need for such activities as knitting or playing ball games. Unlike episodic and semantic knowledge, procedural information is difficult to access and verbalize directly. While you can recall your mother's maiden name from episodic memory, and your concept of a maiden name from semantic memory, you cannot so easily summon and explain the procedural memory that tells you how to drive.

Try describing to someone exactly how you tie shoelaces. Which hand do you start with? What does each finger do? How does each hand hold the laces? Such bundles of knowledge need to be demonstrated not described. They are stored in long-term memory and retrieved just like other memories, yet they are difficult to verbalize as a series of consecutive actions.

As with the other types of long-term memory, procedural memories are never lost. By continually practicing and accumulating procedural information in long-term memory you can improve and develop your physical skills throughout your life.

Misplaced Memories

Everyone forgets information—or so its seems. In fact, the word "forgotten" tends to be used incorrectly to mean "lost from memory," when what it actually describes is a failed attempt at retrieval. When you say you have forgotten a name or a fact, you mean that you cannot recall it from your memory.

Once information has been stored in your long-term memory, it is unlikely to disappear, and may last a lifetime. Even when you cannot recall a name or fact, you can recognize it when you hear it again. "Oh yes, I'd forgotten that!" means you didn't really forget it at all.

It is much easier to learn information the second time, since your memory of it merely needs to be refreshed. By making the information more interesting or by linking it to other information, you are less likely to misplace it in the future. Using a selection of memory tricks (see pages 58 to 99) in this way reduces the likelihood of future retrieval failure.

Lost but not forgotten
Like a book that has fallen from its place on the shelf, a memory can be mislaid. It gathers dust through lack of use, but it is still there waiting to be recalled.

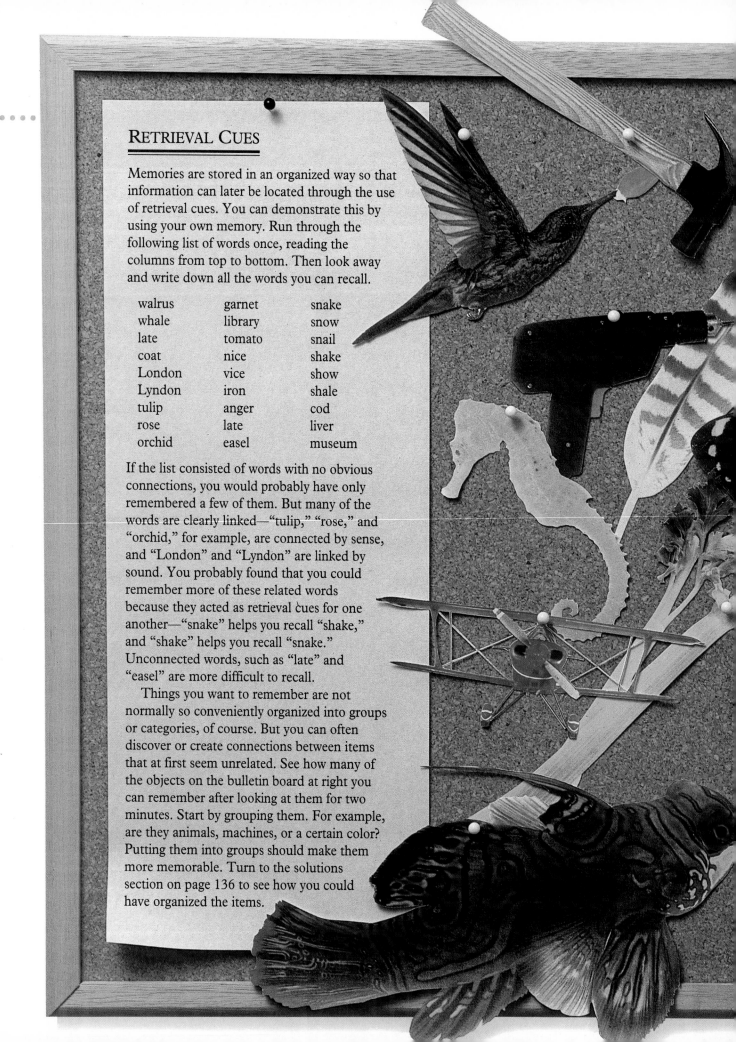

RETRIEVAL CUES

Memories are stored in an organized way so that information can later be located through the use of retrieval cues. You can demonstrate this by using your own memory. Run through the following list of words once, reading the columns from top to bottom. Then look away and write down all the words you can recall.

walrus	garnet	snake
whale	library	snow
late	tomato	snail
coat	nice	shake
London	vice	show
Lyndon	iron	shale
tulip	anger	cod
rose	late	liver
orchid	easel	museum

If the list consisted of words with no obvious connections, you would probably have only remembered a few of them. But many of the words are clearly linked—"tulip," "rose," and "orchid," for example, are connected by sense, and "London" and "Lyndon" are linked by sound. You probably found that you could remember more of these related words because they acted as retrieval cues for one another—"snake" helps you recall "shake," and "shake" helps you recall "snake." Unconnected words, such as "late" and "easel" are more difficult to recall.

Things you want to remember are not normally so conveniently organized into groups or categories, of course. But you can often discover or create connections between items that at first seem unrelated. See how many of the objects on the bulletin board at right you can remember after looking at them for two minutes. Start by grouping them. For example, are they animals, machines, or a certain color? Putting them into groups should make them more memorable. Turn to the solutions section on page 136 to see how you could have organized the items.

SCRIPTS AND SCENARIOS

MUCH OF WHAT IS recalled as memory is not an accurate picture of what happened, but a combination of the real events and information already held about what usually happens in similar circumstances—an expected scenario, which psychologists call a schema or script. Memories can become distorted when the script fills in gaps in the memories, causing inaccurate assumptions about what has been seen, read, or experienced. In other words, part of any memory is likely to have been invented according to your expectations. To understand how this happens, read the following:

When they came back after a long, dusty summer walk, Laura invited her boyfriend in. But when she opened the refrigerator, it was almost empty. "Hmm," thought Laura, "maybe my neighbor can help me out."

Understanding this apparently simple scene requires the mind to unconsciously fill in background detail from its store of general knowledge—semantic memory. Demonstrate this for yourself using the story you have just read. Without rereading it, retell it or write it down. Don't read any farther until you have done this.

When you recalled Laura's story, did you use the words "thirsty" and "drink?" They were not in the story so where did they come from? You reconstructed your memory from a few remembered details along with your knowledge, or script, of a

similar situation: If you had just come in after a long, hot walk, you would be thirsty, and a drink would be uppermost in your mind. You adapted the story to fit your script.

Ground rules

To examine this process in your own life, try to recall an event that took place recently—a meal in a restaurant perhaps. You probably remember entering the restaurant, sitting at a table, and ordering the food. Later, you paid the bill and left. But how much of what you remember is a memory of a particular night and how much is a general memory of what happens in restaurants?

Most of what you recalled was probably reconstructed from your restaurant script. When you could not remember specific details, you made guesses based on your past experience—scripted information. The restaurant script, like every past

Scripted scenes

Use your scripted knowledge of a familiar situation to work out what is happening here. Look at the sequence of pictures on these two pages briefly, and then write down what you can *remember from the four pictures, without looking at them again. Compare your written story with the picture sequence, and then turn to the solutions on page 136.*

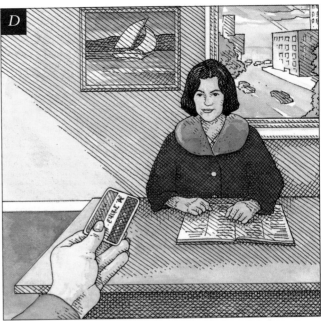

situation you experience frequently, is held in your long-term memory as a sequence of actions in chronological order with a goal—in this case, to eat a meal. What your restaurant script does not contain are the exact details about the decor, the food you ordered, or the bill. These details change, and so cannot be entered into the script.

Scripts are useful for coping with common activities like catching a bus or doing a job, since they hold advance information about what a

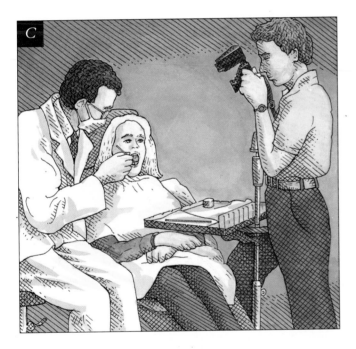

situation is like and what events and people can be expected there. When one part of a situation deviates from the script, the result is a surprise; you wouldn't expect to see a fire fighter in your office.

Scripts also guide communication. If someone remarks, "The food was good, but the service was awful," you know exactly what is meant; your script supplies the waiter's abrupt manner as he takes the order and the long delay before it arrives. Similarly, if someone says, "My doctor was so sympathetic today," you can conjure up the whole scenario. You know your friend went to her doctor's office, had her name called, saw the doctor, the doctor listened carefully to her symptoms and was very helpful. Afterward, she felt relieved. The detail your memory supplied made it possible for you to understand what your friend was saying.

For most everyday situations, the advantages of scripted knowledge are obvious: You know what to expect in familiar situations, can make predictions about novel situations that resemble known ones, and need only devote time and attention to the unusual or distinguishing parts of otherwise routine experiences. But scripted memory also has its drawbacks. Your memories of events can be gradually changed to conform with what you expect rather than what actually happened. Where there are gaps in your memory, you make assumptions based on your expectations. These small changes can gradually distort your memories. The use of scripted knowledge can, for example, lead to many inaccuracies in eyewitness accounts (see "Do you really remember?" on pages 112 to 119).

Biased thinking
People interpret situations in everyday life according to what they already know. What do you think is happening in this picture? Turn to page 137 to see if you are right.

An Eskimo-Indian Folk Tale

One night two young men from Egulac went down to the river to hunt seals. While they were there it became foggy and calm. Then they heard war cries and they thought:

This folk tale—also called the *War of the Ghosts*—was used by British psychologist Sir Frederick Bartlett in a memory study during the 1930s.

"Maybe this is a war party." They escaped to the shore and hid behind a log. Now canoes came up, and they heard the noise of the paddles and saw one canoe coming up to them. There were five men in the canoe, and they said:

"What do you think? We wish to take you along. We are going up the river to make war on the people."

One of the young men said, "I have no arrows."

"Arrows are in the canoe," they said.

"I will not go along. I might be killed. My relatives do not know where I have gone. But you," he said, turning to the other, "may go with them." So one of the young men went, but the other returned home.

And the warriors went on up the river to a town on the other side of Kalama. The people came down to the water, and they began to fight, and many were killed. But presently, the young man heard one of the warriors say, "Quick, let us go home, that Indian has been hit." Now he thought, "Oh, they are ghosts." He did not feel sick, but they said he had been shot.

So the canoes went back to Egulac, and the young man went ashore to his house and made a fire. And he told everybody and said, "Behold I was accompanied by ghosts, and we went off to fight. Many of our fellows were killed, and many of those who attacked us were killed. They said I was hit, and I did not feel sick."

He told it all and then became quiet. When the sun rose he fell down. Something black came out of his mouth. His face became contorted. The people jumped up and cried. He was dead.

Now that you have read this story, write out what you remember of the events it describes without referring back. To see how time affects what you remember, you can repeat this process in a few days. If you are planning to do so, don't read this page yet. Once you have written down your version of the story, check it against the original. Did you lose details or change the story in any way?

One man's version

Here is an example of how one person fared when he was asked to recount the story immediately after reading it once.

"Two Eskimos went to hunt seals one night. While they were out, the night turned foggy and calm. They heard noises, so went back to shore and hid behind a log. There is a canoe full of warriors who say they are going upstream to make war on the Indians and ask the two Eskimos to join them. One of the Eskimos says, 'I have no arrow and my family doesn't know where I am,' and turns to his companion and says, 'But you go.'

"So the younger Eskimo goes with the war party and the fighting begins. Many are killed on both sides. The Eskimo hears his fellow warriors say, 'Stop, we must retreat, he has been hurt,' and he realizes they are referring to him. But he feels fine. The other warriors vanish and he cries, 'They are ghosts.' He then returns to his village, where he recounts the night's events and how he was hit but feels no pain. Suddenly, he falls to the ground and black stuff comes out of his mouth. The villagers pronounce him dead."

Different ideas

This person had a good memory for the story and managed to recall much of it correctly. But, as might be expected, his version is shorter and more generalized than the original, and a few facts such as the names of the Eskimo towns and the number of men in the canoe have been lost.

More important, however, some of the ideas have been changed according to how this individual sees the world. He has assumed that the older Eskimo is the one who makes the decisions. When the Eskimos leave the battle scene, he refers to it as a retreat according to our culture's win-or-lose theory of conflict. He has also adapted the tale to include a particularly Western idea about ghosts—that they vanish. In the original, the ghosts accompany the Eskimo back to his village.

The original story is deliberately unclear in parts. For example, the first paragraph refers to canoes (plural), then to five men in one canoe (singular). When the subjects of Bartlett's experiments retold the story from memory, they tended not only to leave out seemingly unimportant features such as the other canoes, but also to "normalize" the story. These normalizations were in the direction of their own knowledge and beliefs. This tendency was so strong, in fact, that after a few weeks, none of them even remembered the ghosts at all.

Bartlett explained this in terms of scripts (he called them schemas) of knowledge. He found that subjects remembered the story in terms of their own expectations. Their versions were mixtures of the original story together with the knowledge in their own scripts, which had affected their original understanding of what they had read.

VISUAL MEMORY

VISUAL EXPERIENCES dominate most people's lives. During the average 16-hour waking day, the brain is bombarded with an almost continuous array of detailed visual images. Yet only a small proportion of that information is ever stored in memory. The rest can never be recalled, except in only the most general way.

So although your visual memory allows you to recognize a friend you have not seen for 10 years or a scene on television as the place you visited on vacation two years ago, it does not often hold sufficient details to enable you to describe the friend or the spot from memory with any great precision. To remember the specifics of a past visual experience, you must consciously train yourself in the art of paying attention.

Bad penny

Indeed, research has shown that people have a notoriously bad recall of visual detail for even the most common everyday objects. For example, although you would have no difficulty recognizing a penny if you saw one lying on the ground, you probably have little memory for the actual designs on the coin. To prove this to yourself, try drawing both sides of a penny from memory. Be sure to include all words and pictures from the coin. Do not worry about your drawing skills; the sole aim of this exercise is to position the various images and words on the coin correctly.

When you have completed your drawings, check them against the real thing. How many of the following details did you place correctly: The head, the date, the building, and the words "In God We Trust," "Liberty," "United States of America," "E Pluribus Unum," and "One Cent"? Tests have shown that less than one-third of the general population can place the eight critical features of the coin correctly. The average score is three out of eight.

Although the limiting nature of visual memory can be frustrating at

PHOTOGRAPHIC MEMORY

Many young children can summon up an image, such as a drawing from a favorite picture book, and describe it in great detail, as if it were right in front of their eyes. While up to 50 percent of children possess a strong visual memory, only 5 percent have a truly photographic memory. Children tend to lose this ability during their teenage years, and it is rarely found in adults.

You can test someone's claim to have a photographic memory by first asking him or her to read a page of text. Then ask the person to recall that page backward, from the last word to the first. If the person visualized an exact image of the page, he or she should be comfortable recalling it backward as well as forward.

times, it serves a very practical purpose. If you were to remember all the details of everything you saw, your mind would soon become so cluttered with minutiae that it would be difficult for you to attach meaning to anything. Instead, you store only enough of the visual properties of various objects to enable you to make the gross distinctions required to understand the objects' place and purpose in everyday life. To properly use a coin, for example, all you normally need to know is its size and color. If, for any reason, you want to remember the coin in vivid detail, you must make a conscious effort to study it.

The same is true for other objects or pictures. Although general impressions are usually easy to recall, remembering the image in more detail requires a purposeful effort. You must pay attention and carefully examine the object or picture when you first view it.

You use the information stored in your visual memory every day to recognize hundreds of objects and people. You automatically search your memory for an image that matches what

Picture this

Those rare individuals with the gift of photographic memory can recall any picture they have seen—such as the Mona Lisa, for example—as a precise and detailed image. They can then examine different areas of the picture in their mind, homing in on a feature at will, such as a hand or a single eye.

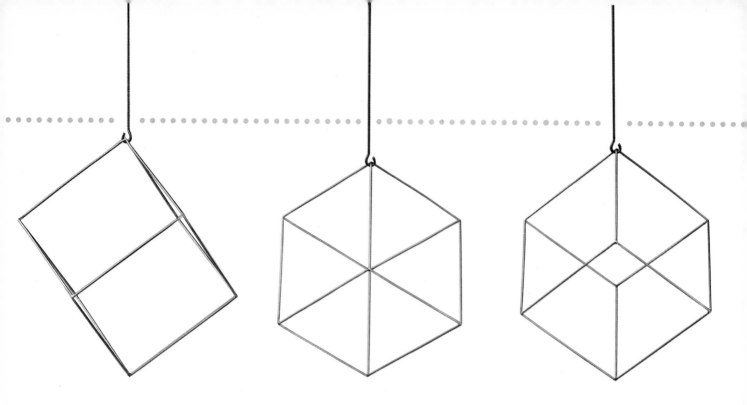

you see. When you find a match, you recognize the object. Research has shown that some types of visual images are easier to recognize than others. In one study, subjects were shown pictures of faces, snowflake patterns, and ink blots, each for only a few seconds. Immediately afterward, they were asked to pick out the images they had just seen from a mixture of pictures that included many new ones of a similar kind. The faces were recognized with 71 percent accuracy, the ink blots with 48 percent accuracy, and the snowflake patterns with 33 percent accuracy. These findings suggest, not surprisingly, that the more meaningful the image the more likely it will be recognized.

Altered images

Remembrances of visual images are not always accurate, however. It is this failing of your visual memory that often accounts for those irritating occasions when you cannot find something you are looking for, even when it is in plain view. You start the search with an image of the missing object in your mind, but because your memory does not recall details of the object, that image is strikingly inaccurate. As a result, you fail to recognize the object during your search, even when your eyes pass over it. You will not, for example, be able to find an orange book if the image you mistakenly conjure up is that of a blue book. To resolve this problem, get in the habit of paying more attention to your surroundings so that your visual memory for detail becomes more accurate.

You may also fail to recognize a familiar object because your visual memory of it is from a specific

Insufficient data

You recognize a shape by comparing it with images in your visual memory store. You may only see this revolving shape as a cube in the third picture, because the first two views do not correspond to your mental image of a cube.

orientation—say from a frontal view—and the object may not be lying in that position. You may not be able to find a book that has been placed upright on the shelf, for example, because your mental image of the book is of its front cover, not of its binding. To find a misplaced object, therefore, try imagining it from different angles.

The ability to conjure up a visual image from memory greatly enhances a person's ability to comprehend written material. Read, for example, the following passage from Ernest Hemingway's *The Snows of Kilimanjaro.*

"Out of the window of the hospital you could see a field with tumbleweed coming out of the snow, and a bare clay butte. From the other window, if the bed was turned, you could see the town, with a little smoke above it, and the Dawson mountains looking like real mountains with the winter snow on them."

As you read these words you probably constructed a mental image of the setting they describe, calling on your visual memory of tumbleweed, snow, mountains, and so on. Without this ability, your imaginative life would be impoverished.

The mind often organizes visual memories three-dimensionally, making it possible for you to

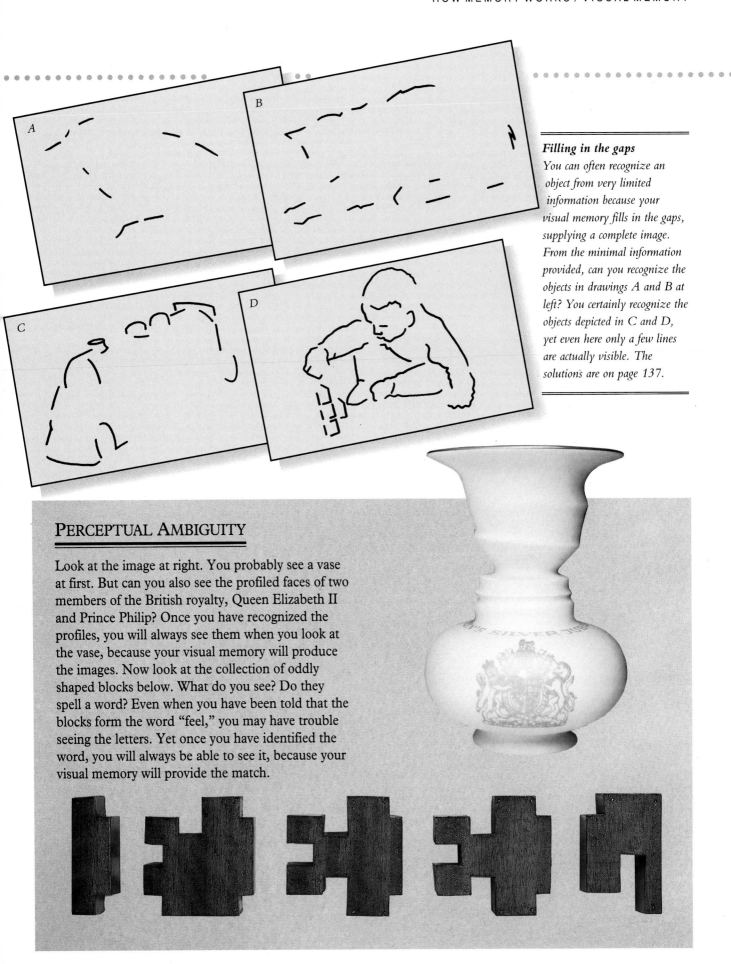

Filling in the gaps
You can often recognize an object from very limited information because your visual memory fills in the gaps, supplying a complete image. From the minimal information provided, can you recognize the objects in drawings A and B at left? You certainly recognize the objects depicted in C and D, yet even here only a few lines are actually visible. The solutions are on page 137.

PERCEPTUAL AMBIGUITY

Look at the image at right. You probably see a vase at first. But can you also see the profiled faces of two members of the British royalty, Queen Elizabeth II and Prince Philip? Once you have recognized the profiles, you will always see them when you look at the vase, because your visual memory will produce the images. Now look at the collection of oddly shaped blocks below. What do you see? Do they spell a word? Even when you have been told that the blocks form the word "feel," you may have trouble seeing the letters. Yet once you have identified the word, you will always be able to see it, because your visual memory will provide the match.

MAP OUT YOUR WORLD

How accurate is your mental map of the United States? Find out for yourself. Take a blank piece of paper and put a dot on it to represent the town you live in. Don't draw an outline on your map of the United States; instead, simply position the following cities at a suitable distance and direction from your home town: New York, Boston, Atlanta, Miami, New Orleans, Houston, Detroit, Washington D.C., Dallas, Minneapolis, Seattle, Los Angeles, San Diego, Denver, Phoenix, San Francisco, Kansas City, Memphis, Indianapolis, and Chicago.

Then, using your placement of the cities as a guide, draw in the outline of the United States. Compare what you have drawn with the map on page 138.

Did you unconsciously distort the distances between the cities, and thus end up with a distorted shape for the country? Places nearer to you seem more important; thus you probably exaggerated the distances between cities closer to home and decreased the distances between those farther away.

Inaccurate mental maps

Research shows that, when asked to draw a map of their home country from memory, people exaggerate the size of the area in which they themselves live. A southern *Italian might exaggerate the size of the toe and heel of Italy (above, left), whereas a person living in the north would do the opposite (above, right).*

Are you sharp-eyed?

One of the most effective tests of visual memory is the famous "spot-the-difference" type of puzzle. Look at the picture on the left for 30 seconds. Then turn to page 47 and see if you can spot the differences in the second version of this picture from memory.

remember the position of objects in a room, for example, that are not directly in your line of view as you "look" upon the room in your memory. This spatial awareness occurs in the memory even if the remembered room is not experienced first-hand, but merely through a suggestive description. Read the following description and imagine yourself in the scene: You are at the opera. You are standing next to a balcony railing. Directly behind you, mounted on a nearby wall, is a lamp. You see a large bronze plaque on the wall to your left. On a shelf directly to your right is a bouquet of flowers.

Now, imagine yourself slowly turning 90 degrees in a clockwise direction. Where would you have to look to see the bouquet of flowers? And where, relative to you, is the plaque? By imagining yourself in the scene you can probably easily work out that the flowers are now directly in front of you and the plaque behind you. Research has shown that, when remembering themselves in a scene, it takes people more time to locate something behind them than ahead of them, perhaps because they have to imagine turning around.

Route memory
The ability to hold a visual image of a place in your head helps you find your way around a familiar environment, like your home or workplace. Using visual clues stored in your memory, you could probably safely navigate through your home

TEST YOUR LOCAL KNOWLEDGE

Imagine that you have a visitor from out of town staying with you who wants to go to the local library. He says he is the sort of person who easily gets lost and asks you to draw a map for him showing what roads he should take, the junctions he will pass, and the buildings or other visual reference points along the route that mark the turns he should make.

Try drawing him a map from memory. Make sure that you have given sufficient visual references and marked any public buildings, rivers, or railways he is likely to pass on the way. Then check the accuracy of your drawing against a local map. You may be surprised to find that, although you would have no difficulty at all finding the way yourself, your map is only a very approximate representation of the actual situation.

The next time you use the route, pay more attention to the road layout, and look at the buildings or landmarks to see which ones you omitted.

How did I get there?
Most people carry simple route maps in their memories that enable them to navigate familiar journeys. These mental maps use landmarks as clues, but are often simplified and full of gaps.

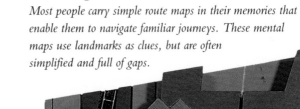

TEST YOUR VISUAL MEMORY

The ability to conjure up visual memories varies among individuals. Women report more vivid and more frequent memory images than do men. In one study, for example, more than three-quarters of the women surveyed agreed with the statement, "I often remember work I have studied by imagining the page on which it is written." Among the men surveyed, only about half said they agreed with the statement. Most people of either sex, however, have difficulty recalling visual details, even of familiar objects that they think they know well. To test your own visual memory, look at the four items shown here. Can you identify the missing element from each of these well-known images? The solutions can be found on page 139.

Spot the difference
You have looked at the picture on page 44 for 30 seconds. Now, without looking back, compare this picture with your memory of the first version. Write down any differences you find between them. Once you have done this, turn to the solutions on page 138 to check your answers.

in the dark. You also use visual memories to find your way around your neighborhood or town. When driving to a friend's house, for example, you know to turn right at the street after the service station—even if you haven't memorized the name of the street or of the service station.

Committing an unfamiliar route to memory, on the other hand, always poses a problem. To increase your chances of remembering a new route, look for visual references at each turn you make. Once you have identified your visual clues, you can develop a rhyme to help you remember them, such as "Left at the lights, right at the white [building]." Also, be sure to look back occasionally at your visual references as you travel along a route for the first time. This will help you recognize the references from the other direction on your return journey. Where possible, use a tall familiar building as a reference point. If, for example, you emerge from a shopping center by an unusual exit and need to reorient yourself, you can use the large reference point to find more familiar territory.

Most people's memorized routes cover only a relatively small geographic area around their home or workplace. More distant routes, as well as the relative locations of various faraway geographic

sites, are learned by studying maps. Yet people's mental images of maps tend to be very general, just like their memories of other pictures. Relying too heavily on a mental memory of a map, therefore, can lead to errors. For example, which of the following statements, if any, are true?
• Madrid, Spain, is farther north than Washington, D.C.
• Seattle, Washington, is farther north than Montreal, Canada.
• The Pacific entrance of the Panama Canal is east of the Atlantic entrance.

In fact, all of these statements are true. Without referring to a map, many people think they are false because they judge the relative positions of the places by comparing larger geographic units—countries, states, or oceans—of which they have a clearer visual memory. Canada, for example, is remembered as being north of the United States, so it seems Montreal must be north of Seattle.

Some people possess a stronger visual memory than others. Yet, everyone can improve their visual memory with a little effort. If you wish to recall an object or scene accurately, take time to examine it carefully. Pay attention to details. When this becomes a habit, your visual memory will improve.

THE POWER OF CONTEXT

STRANGE BUT TRUE: If you learn something while in the bath, you'll have an easier time recalling it when you have a soak again. Experts call this syndrome "context dependency," and they have found it to be a powerful memory aid. In fact, the syndrome's potential for improving memory has yet to be fully exploited and could challenge many established learning techniques.

Psychologists have observed that if you learn something in a certain place or environment, you are more likely to remember it if you are in that same place or environment. In other words, the context in which you learn something has a great bearing on the likelihood of recall. You will probably be familiar with one or all of the following cases:

• Upon your return to a certain building or town that you have not visited for many years, you remember events and feelings you had not recollected since you were last there.

• You are at work and walk right by someone without recognizing him or her. The person turns out to be from your neighborhood and just happens to be visiting your place of work.

• You excel in a course that teaches you a skill that is valuable to your job, but when you return to the workplace, you find you cannot perform the skill as well as you did in the classroom.

Out of place
As the last two of these examples illustrate, context dependency can actually impede your memory as well as help it. If you are more used to seeing your neighbor Bill washing his car in his overalls, it can take quite a bit of effort to recognize him out of that context, such as when he appears before you at work wearing a suit and carrying a briefcase. In a similar way, new skills learned away from the work site can be difficult to apply at the same level of proficiency that you achieved during the training course.

The importance of context is not a new discovery. The British philosopher John Locke recognized and chronicled it as long ago as 1690. He

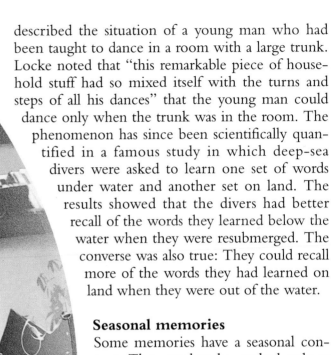

described the situation of a young man who had been taught to dance in a room with a large trunk. Locke noted that "this remarkable piece of household stuff had so mixed itself with the turns and steps of all his dances" that the young man could dance only when the trunk was in the room. The phenomenon has since been scientifically quantified in a famous study in which deep-sea divers were asked to learn one set of words under water and another set on land. The results showed that the divers had better recall of the words they learned below the water when they were resubmerged. The converse was also true: They could recall more of the words they had learned on land when they were out of the water.

Seasonal memories

Some memories have a seasonal context: They tend to be evoked only at certain times of the year. At Christmas, for example, you may suddenly recall the sights and smells of past Christmas dinners or the memory of receiving a favorite toy. Or in early June, when the days are long and the air warm, you may recollect the joy and freedom of childhood summer vacations, perhaps even a long-forgotten special summer when you first learned how to ride a bike or made a new friend.

You don't necessarily need to return to a particular environment or setting, however, to experience the power of context-dependency as a memory aid. Research has shown that your memory can be successfully triggered by simply imagining yourself back in the environment in which you learned the information you

Being there

Memories are often context-dependent. The mind does not remember facts and feelings in isolation, but rather as part of the environment in which the information was initially absorbed. So returning to that environment, your old bedroom for example, whether physically or in the imagination, can provide a cue to recall the original information.

A NOSE FOR THE PAST

A distinctive smell or taste can evoke a memory with great clarity. Researchers sometimes refer to this phenomenon as "Proustian memory," after the French novelist Marcel Proust. In Proust's most famous novel, *Remembrance of Things Past*, the narrator recalls his childhood vacations in detail after tasting madeleine cake soaked in lime tea—a taste he had last experienced at that early time of his life.

"Proustian memory" is often associated with "synesthesia," a crossing over between two different senses. Many people have mild synesthetic experiences. For example, a person who smells a red rose at the same time that he first hears a particular song might subsequently experience a vivid recall of the smell each time he later encounters the tune.

People who routinely experience sensory crossovers in everyday life are called synesthetes. Some of them see names and sounds as particular colors, a phenomenon which can greatly help their efforts at recall: "She had a green name—so it was either Karen or Cheryl. It couldn't be Jennifer because to me that is definitely a purple name." Do you ever see names in color?

wish to remember. This suggests a useful tip: When trying to recall something, first make an effort to remember the surroundings in which you learned the information. If you are trying to recall how your mother made her well-loved turkey dressing, for example, try imagining yourself back in her kitchen. Or if you need help recalling first-aid information you learned in a course, envision yourself in the classroom and recall how everything looked as the information was presented.

State dependence

It is not only the external environment that provides cues for recall. Our internal environment, including our moods, can also have this effect. Experiences encountered while in an alcoholic stupor, for example, are best remembered when in an alcoholic stupor. The term "state-dependent memory" has been coined to describe this syndrome. The idea was used to great effect in the movie *City Lights*, starring Charlie Chaplin. In the film, Chaplin saves a drunken millionaire from committing suicide, and the millionaire befriends him. Once sober, however, the millionaire does not remember who Chaplin is. However, when the man gets drunk again, he spots Chaplin and treats him like a long-lost friend, taking him home and insisting he stay as a guest. In the morning, though, the effects of alcohol have worn off, and Chaplin is once again unrecognizable to the millionaire, who promptly throws him out of the house.

Although the practical applications of learning and recalling while drunk are limited, the fact that your inner state—most specifically, your mood—influences what you can remember does have widespread implications. One of the many negative aspects of being depressed, for example, is that it tends to bring on memories of other times when you were depressed,

PUT YOURSELF IN PLACE

Everyone has at one time or another experienced the annoyance of losing or mislaying an everyday object, such as a set of keys, a wallet or purse, or the dog's leash. Most people have also encountered the common frustration of walking into a room at home or at work, then puzzling over why they wanted to be there.

To help yourself in these situations, you need to put yourself back in the environment in which you first misplaced the object or lost your train of thought. The best way to do that is by retracing your steps. For example, when you can't find your house keys one morning, try reenacting your homecoming the previous evening. Physically mimic your actions: Stand outside the front door, pretend to put the keys in the locks, and step inside. Then take off your coat, check the mail, switch on the television, or do whatever else you might have done on your return the night before. You might feel foolish going through these motions, but by recreating your actions in context, your memories will be that much more accessible. You will then be more likely to distill memories of that particular evening from the composite memory of similar evenings—and be able to locate your lost keys.

Delving deep
The effects of context-dependent memory were tested on deep-sea divers, who were given words to learn either under 15 feet of water or on the beach. Their recall for both lists was then tested in both environments. The results showed that the divers had a much better memory of each list when they were asked to recall it in the same environment in which it had been taught.

thus adding to your feeling of sadness. Conversely, a happy mood will trigger memories of past joyful times. Thus your mood affects your memory, which, in turn, can further affect your mood.

State-dependent memory may also be involved in the relationship between cigarette smoking and recall. People who smoke claim that they are better able to concentrate when smoking, and tests have indeed shown that nicotine focuses the mind. Researchers have also found that information learned while smoking is easier to recall when smoking again. These findings may partly explain why so many people report that their work suffers when they finally manage to quit smoking. With their memories dependent on the state of smoking,

they may indeed have trouble recalling information that came quite easily to them when they were still puffing on cigarettes.

You can use context dependency and state dependency to aid your memory: Remember that you are more likely to recall information when you are in the same situation that you learned it. You can also reap the benefits of the phenomenon by recreating original learning situations in your mind. Remember, however, that when the differences between the learning and recalling environments are not great, the context-dependent effect is negligible. So there is no need to worry if you are, say, taking tests in a different hall from the one in which you attended your lectures.

REMEMBER YOURSELF

WHEN YOU CHANCE UPON an old snapshot in a drawer, you may find memories flooding back. You suddenly recall that warm evening in the backyard, the friends gathered at the barbecue, and the state of your life at that time. Yet it is just as possible that the photo will reveal huge gaps in your memory: Who was that person with his arm around your shoulder? And what was the occasion of the gathering? Your memories from your past life may seem remarkably patchy, with the occasional brightly illuminated scene surrounded by areas of impenetrable darkness.

Research suggests that most individuals are able to recall about 200 personal incidents from the most recent 20 years of their lives. This came to be known as "Galton's number," in tribute to the English psychologist Sir Francis Galton, the man who first tried to measure autobiographical memory. Mathematically, Galton's number works out to an average of about 10 remembered events per year. Those memories, however, are not evenly distributed over the 20 years. The frequency of personal memories decreases as a function of how long ago they occurred. So, according to this research, there are probably entire years in your life from which you can recall only one or two events, or none at all.

Early days

Many people have a well-polished account of their "first memory"—whether it is sitting in a baby buggy, a first day at kindergarten, or moving into a new house at about two years of age. These first memories are almost impossible to verify because they might have been suggested by a photograph or an overheard adult conversation.

Typically, a person's earliest memory will be from when he or she was three or four years old. Few people can remember events from before that age. Although scientists remain undecided about the reason for this lack of early memories, they have offered three main theories. Some believe that the very young child's brain pathways, which are

Memory milestones
Important events in your life, such as graduating from high school or getting married, act as memory milestones to which you can relate other events.

Physical objects—a diploma or wedding gown, for example—also act as powerful retrieval cues for recalling those important moments.

vital for mem-
ory, are not yet
completely formed. Others
hypothesize that memories
cannot take a recognizable form
until a child has a grasp of language. Still other researchers believe
that the adult's perception of the world
is so different from that of a child, that
access to early memories becomes lost forever once a person ages.

The ability to remember an event seems to
depend on how much emotional importance it
carries and on how rare an event it is. You will not
recall the details of a commonplace day from your
childhood, but the day your baseball team won the
city championship will stand out in sharp relief.
Psychologists have even found that partial amnesia
occurs concerning details immediately before a
major event, as if the brightness of this event casts a
shadow over neighboring memories.

Most people would love to bring more of their
personal memories out of the shadows, and to

I REMEMBER YESTERDAY

When left to free-associate, most people tend to arrange their personal memories under traditional headings like school days, birthdays, wedding days, and holidays. A good way to produce a fuller, more detailed autobiographical memory is to use a cuing technique. By reading a prepublished list of everyday objects and thinking of a personal memory for each one, you can force your mind to access your memories from unusual angles, which might prompt the resurgence of unusual personal recollections. Using the following list of 20 words as prompts, write down a personal memory for each one. Try to give each remembered episode a date. For example, for "carrot" you might recall the time last summer when you cut your finger shredding carrots for a salad at a lunch party. Using this technique, you may find new chapters of your life suddenly open up to you.

Carrot	Blanket	Tree	Door
Haircut	Spoon	Ink	Telephone
Parakeet	Glass	Cat	Garage
Clock	Wire	Bottle	Bucket
Grass	Dictionary	Sand	Mixing bowl

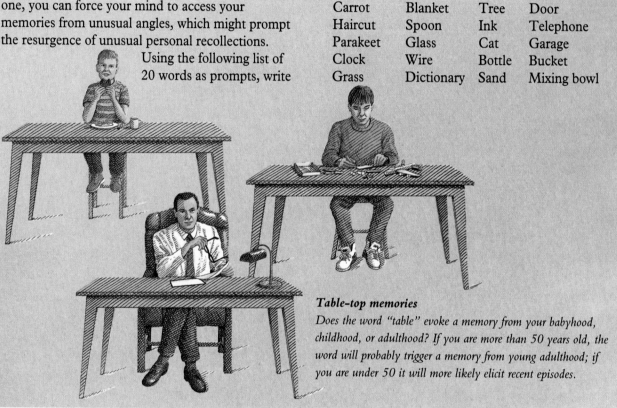

Table-top memories
Does the word "table" evoke a memory from your babyhood, childhood, or adulthood? If you are more than 50 years old, the word will probably trigger a memory from young adulthood; if you are under 50 it will more likely elicit recent episodes.

develop a clear and detailed picture of their past experiences. This is why the snapshot and home video industries exist. People want to store their memories and relive them later. But, short of keeping every day of your life on tape, what can you do to improve your recall of your life?

Dragging your past life out of the shadows requires a systematic effort. You will need to apply the fundamental memory principle of association. This technique enables one memory to pull another with it, providing more and more hooks for further retrieval. Start with any clues to your past. Dig out old photographs, copies of letters, diaries you may have written, or even official documents. Use each one of these as a starting point for a memory trip. Where were you when the letter was written? Who sent it to you and what was your relationship to that person at the time? How much can you

recall of your circumstances then? Feel your way back into the period. Jot down the things you remember, so they are not lost again.

Hold these memory sessions regularly—about once a week for an hour is ideal—and see if you can begin to create a more complete autobiography. Search out clues to fill in the blanks where your memory is weakest. As linked sets of memories accumulate, you will find that fresh memories begin to appear unsought in your mind. You will also discover that your overall remembrance of things past may be permanently improved.

Of course, your memory of the events of your past life may not always be accurate. Your autobiographical memories are shaped by the image you have of yourself and by your feelings of self-importance. In psychological experiments where subjects were asked to take part in a group task and then to describe what happened some time later, most of them exaggerated the importance of their own contribution to the task, although they were trying to be honest. Experiments have also shown, however, that people's recall for personal events is generally true in outline; that is, it is not substantially misleading, even if the details are distorted.

Historical memory

You are unlikely to be able to date your personal memories clearly unless they are linked to public events. You find yourself saying, for example, "We must have last met in 1988 because I remember that President Bush had just been elected," or "Yes, I remember exactly when I started that job because it was the same month that my home team, the Minnesota Twins, won the World Series."

To look at the interrelationship between historical and personal memories, try this test. Decide whether the following events happened during the Carter or Reagan administrations. Then read the lists again and write down what you were doing in your personal life at the time each event occurred:

Argentina invades the Falklands; the Ayatollah Khomeini takes over in Iran; Egyptian President Sadat is assassinated; the Soviet Union invades Afghanistan; Margaret Thatcher first becomes British prime minister; 911 people die in Jonestown suicides; Elvis Presley dies; Jimmy Connors wins Wimbledon; Pope John Paul is wounded in Rome; Prince Charles marries Lady Diana Spencer. (The answers are on page 139.)

You probably found that you could classify the purely political events, such as the Argentinian invasion, fairly quickly in terms of the presidency in which they occurred. Nonpolitical events are harder to classify in these terms.

Overall, however, autobiographical memory involves a quite complex interrelationship between public and private events. Nowhere is this relationship more apparent than in "flashbulb memories," those memories in which shocking, momentous public events are inextricably linked to personal remembrances.

A TRUE RECORD?

John Dean was one of President Richard Nixon's lawyers during the early 1970s, the period leading up to the Watergate scandal. The accuracy of his memory concerning the Watergate events therefore became a matter of national importance. Dean apparently became convinced that he was being set up as a scapegoat in the case and turned against the White House. His voluminous and detailed testimony at Senate hearings undermined Nixon's credibility and was an important factor leading to the president's resignation. Because many of the White House conversations had been taped, it was possible to check the accuracy of much of Dean's recall.

Comparing accounts

The tapes revealed that Dean was falsely confident when he recalled details of conversations. Occasionally he would present what appeared to be verbatim recollections of conversations, but these turned out to be inaccurate. While Dean's memory was false in specific parts, however, it was true as a general whole. His overall impression of Nixon's behavior was found to be correct.

John Dean's experience shows that although most people's autobiographical memories may not be literally correct, they may nonetheless be true in a wider sense.

It has become a cliché to observe that people who were at least of school age when President John Kennedy was assassinated are able to recall in detail the moment they became aware of the event. Researchers have described this phenomenon as a form of mental photocopying; the mind takes and preserves a detailed rendition of an original event. Yet, although such memories appear to remain clear and unchanged, research does suggest that even they are susceptible to distortion and forgetting through the passage of time.

Memory studies were conducted after the *Challenger* space-shuttle explosion of January 28, 1986. People were asked to recount their detailed recollections of the event both three days and nine months after the disaster. Discrepancies between the two sets of memories were common. People who said they were in one place when they heard about the disaster (for example, coming down the stairs at school), nine months later recalled being in quite another place (for example, in a classroom). The nine-month-old memories also contained less detail. These results suggest that flashbulb memories are not necessarily accurate, despite their vividness. Can you remember what you were doing when you heard the news of the *Challenger* disaster? If you have a distinct memory, check it with someone else who was with you at the time, to see whether your memories match.

Keep track of your life
The kinds of momentous public events that enable people to remember private experiences do not, fortunately, happen all that often. As aids to creating more detailed autobiographical memories, they are, at best, unreliable. You can, however, take steps to create better memories of your life. Above all, keep a diary. As a source of future recall it can't be beat. When you read it later, you will remember much more than is actually recorded in each entry. Include events from the news, to link your personal and public memories. Few experiences are more rewarding than meditating on your past, and such practice automatically improves recall.

LEAVING AN IMPRESSION

The study of flashbulb memories has often focused on tragic public events, such as the assassinations of John Kennedy and Martin Luther King, Jr., or the *Challenger* space-shuttle disaster. However, scientists now understand that flashbulb memories are also generated by any event that might be a personal shock, one that took you by surprise and had important personal implications. Such events leave a clear, detailed image of where you were and what happened to you at one point in your life— such as the time a sibling was born, or the day you met your movie idol, or the time you won the company football pool.

In the spotlight
Flashbulb memories, where details of a particularly memorable event stay with you in vivid clarity, are as likely to be about a happy personal event as a national disaster. The greater the personal impact of the occasion, the more memorable it will be.

CLEARING YOUR MIND

In an effort to recall deeply embedded memories, especially childhood memories, many people turn to hypnosis. They hope to free their subconscious mind and gain clues about the reasons for their behavior. Although the validity of hypnosis remains controversial, the results obtained under a hypnotist's suggestion can be startling, and are often practical. For example, police sometimes seek the help of hypnotists to prod eyewitnesses into remembering a detail from a crime scene, such as the color of a car or the number on a license plate.

Hypnosis has highlighted the phenomenal capacity of long-term memory by demonstrating how even the briefest of experiences can leave a permanent impression. For instance, some people under hypnosis have come up with detailed accounts of a previous existence in another historical epoque. These memories often turn out to be traceable to movies, pictures, or books that the person has fleetingly seen or read long ago. Hypnosis unlocks this information that has been buried in the long-term memory for decades, and the patient retells events as if he or she experienced them personally.

These memories are not evidence of reincarnation, but of the extraordinary detail of past experience stored in the depths of our minds.

Ultimately, the interpretation of hypnotically induced memories is everything. When questioned under hypnosis in one study, people who had never previously claimed any knowledge of UFOs gave detailed accounts of close encounters with aliens. Research Professor Alvin Lawson of California State University believed that these accounts were fantasized sequences based on people's memories of their own births. He compared the descriptions of contact with aliens with the births each person had experienced. Those born by cesarean section did not refer to the tunnel imagery commonly used by those who had been born naturally, and one subject who had been born by forceps delivery even talked about being "pulled on board" the alien spaceship.

CHAPTER TWO

MEMORY TRICKS

SOME PEOPLE SEEM to be born with a knack for calling to mind names, faces, phone numbers, birth dates, and the scattered impressions of sundry experiences many months in the past. Most of us, however, do not share this gift, and the abilities of people with superior memories can sometimes seem to border on the mystical. In some cases, extraordinary powers of memory are indeed a gift, but perhaps just as often they are the product of single-minded effort and training.

Assiduous adherence to a few straightforward principles can make a tremendous difference to the amount of factual material you can retain. One such principle instructs that if you can make things pithy or fun, they will be easier to remember. The market-savvy journalists of the tabloid *New York Post* followed this dictum when they crafted the "Headless Body in Topless Bar" headline for a lurid story about a murder in a striptease joint. The wordplay in this description probably lingered in the minds of many potential newspaper-buying customers.

Another principle to note is that things that make sense are easier to remember than things that do not. To this end, there is even a way to change numbers into words, so you can, for example, convert a string of digits like 900587112 into letters that read "puzzled kitten," which is, of course, much easier to remember.

This chapter examines a variety of memory techniques, including the use of visualization to link disparate facts in your mind and ways to color plain words to make them vibrant and unforgettable. Even practicing a single new method can bolster your ability to memorize. Armed with a whole range of techniques, committing to memory a list of 30 words or a 20-digit number can suddenly become a simple task, and phone numbers will stay in your head as reliably as they do in the book you keep at home.

Before you judge any of the techniques in this book, remember that memory tricks are rarely sophisticated. Indeed, their effectiveness is often based on a certain childlike quality. Be reassured, however: In their simplicity lies their strength. With the proper assortment of memory tools at your disposal, you can conquer every memory problem you encounter.

YOU CAN ENJOY THE FLAIR AND RESOURCEFULNESS OF A FIRST-RATE MEMORY BY MASTERING A RANGE OF SIMPLE BUT POWERFUL TECHNIQUES.

WORKING MNEMONICS

I N THE COURSE OF A typical afternoon, your friend may mention a great new place for lunch, your boss may drop the name of a potential business contact, and your child may tell you he needs to take a bulb into school for nature class the next day. Information that is useful or important to remember presents itself in many different circumstances—and not just when you are actively seeking it out. Often, however, the information is difficult to recall even a few hours later. The key to holding onto such randomly acquired data—or to highly useful scraps of knowledge that you want to remember years from now—is to invoke a few well-chosen mnemonics, or memory tricks.

You probably already know some of these devices. Most people were drilled at school to use "i before e except after c," when spelling words like "ceiling," and "receive." Likewise, you may have been taught to remember that port, not starboard, is the left side of a boat by noting that both "port" and "left" are four-letter words. By learning the techniques that make such tricks work you can improve your recall ability.

Techniques to adapt

Everything from rhymes, images, acrostics, and acronyms, to codes, stories, and jokes can serve as mnemonics. And the guiding principle in developing your own memory tricks is to use whatever works best for you. Be mindful, however, that there are three main tried-and-true principles of learning—repetition, association, and visualization—that are worth understanding fully. These three techniques can be harnessed for daily use in bolstering your memory.

The simplest and most obvious way to learn something is to repeat it. If you have had training in a foreign language, you have probably had the experience of listening to an instructor pronounce a phrase and then being asked to repeat it over and over until the new words have a chance to take root in your memory.

Pulling out facts

Like a magnet extracting metal from a general mix of other materials, association makes it possible to recall hard-to-remember facts. The trick is to link the new facts to data that is already well-known.

Learning by rote also enters into many other types of study—particularly around exam time, when hundreds of facts are studied for brief periods. Moreover, this same approach is often adopted outside the context of schooling. If you are given an important phone number at a moment when there is no pencil handy, you will probably chant the number to yourself in order not to forget it.

Repetition, therefore, does have its uses. But it is hardly sufficient in itself, and—as any school-child will gladly tell you—it is a boring way to learn. The ideal recipe for memorization is to come up with some sort of mnemonic and then reinforce it through repetition.

Forming associations

Because two related items are easier to remember than two unrelated ones, association is a formidable tool for improving memory. One application for this technique is to help you keep straight the meaning of similar-sounding words. Take the names of those icicle-like rock formations found in some caves, stalagmites and stalactites. How can you remember which one grows up and which one comes down? The two words are easily confused until you find associations that will help you differentiate their meanings. You can associate stala**c**tites with the **c**eiling, to which they cling so tightly; stala**g**mites, on the other hand, grow up from the **g**round, or the floor of the cave.

In that example, you used associated ideas to help you remember the meanings of words. It is also possible to use associated words to help you remember ideas. For instance, one of the principal differences between African and Indian elephants is that the African species has larger ears. A zoologist, therefore, might rely on a mnemonic phrase that makes use of the initial letters of each species in order to remember the size difference: **A**frican ele-phants **all** have **a**mple ears, while those from **In**dia are **in**significant.

LEARN JAPANESE

If you are learning a foreign language, you may find association particularly helpful for memorizing new vocabulary.

Listed below are the numbers from one to 10 in Japanese. Study them in pairs—one and two together, three and four, and so on. Then, based on what the words sound like, make a mental association for each pair: "Ichi nee," for instance, could become "itchy knee," which you might envision as a man scratching his knee. "San she" might become "sand she," with an image of a girl buried under sand, while "Go roku" sounds like "go rock you," perhaps a cradle on wheels or a rock-and-roll guitarist.

Using this method, you may be surprised at how quickly you can learn all 10 numbers—and at how well the memory sticks.

1 ICHI	*2 NEE*
3 SAN	*4 SHE*
5 GO	*6 ROKU*
7 NANA	*8 HACHI*
9 Q	*10 JU*

MERCURY ● VENUS ● EARTH ● MARS ● JUPITER

PLANETARY TRICKS

One quick way to learn the names of the planets and the order in which they circle the sun—Mercury, Venus, Earth, Mars, Jupiter, Saturn, Uranus, Neptune, Pluto—is to memorize the sentence (technically an acrostic) "My Very Educated Mother Just Served Us Nine Pumpkins." This mnemonic not only distinguishes

Mercury from Mars (by including the letter "y" in "My") but also reminds you there are nine planets in all by including the word "nine."

For the more dramatic-minded, there is an alternative. Another way to learn the same information is to create a short play which features each planet, either as a character or as a prop. Here is an example:

Association is particularly helpful with troublesome spellings. Linking the spelling to the meaning, you can help yourself remember the first "a" in "separate," by reminding yourself that the meaning of the word is "to part." Another spelling trick is to associate the words with simpler words contained within them: If you int**err**upt, you will **err**, and you will **miss** out if you **miss**pell. In the pages that follow, you will find a variety of ways to use association for overcoming special problems, such as remembering birthdays, names, and numbers.

Organization helps

Just as it is easier to find things in your kitchen if they are put away according to a system—silverware in the counter drawer, pots and pans in the right-hand cupboard—so it is easier to absorb information once it has been organized in some form or fashion. When you are presented with anything new, in fact, your mind will generally attempt to group it with some existing pattern of information already well understood. Here is a simple example of the power of organization:

Study the following 13 random letters for one minute: DPHYBTYHPIARA. When you have done so, close the book, and attempt to write down the letters in any order.

Not that easy is it? Without organization, recalling these 13 random letters is an onerous memory task. But if you had been given the fact that this string of letters was an anagram of "happy birthday," you would have had no difficulty in remembering the letters. Once information is organized, the job of remembering is largely done.

The rhymes and rhythms of verse can also be put to use in providing a context for information you

RHYMES AND KNUCKLES

Jingles and rhymes are often useful for memorizing facts or names. Most people, for instance, are familiar with the rhyme for remembering the number of days in each month:

Thirty days hath September,
April, June, and November.
All the rest have 31,
Except February alone,
Which has but 28 days clear,
And 29 in each leap year.

JANUARY   MARCH   MAY   JULY
FEBRUARY   APRIL   JUNE

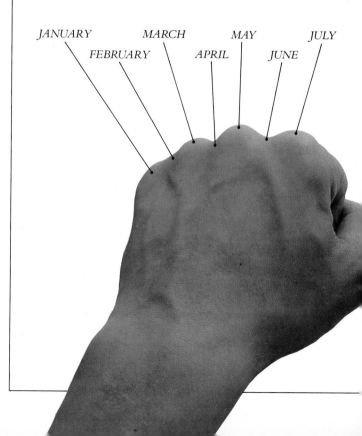

SATURN   URANUS   NEPTUNE   PLUTO

A broken thermometer scatters balls of **Mercury** across the floor. A beautiful woman, **Venus,** comes to pick up the balls. In trying to pick the mercury from the floor she gets **Earth** trapped under her fingernails. This makes her boyfriend, **Mars,** angry. "By **Jupiter**!" he exclaims, "You are a mess." He is disappointed because he wanted her to look good for their date on **Satur[n]**day night. Outraged at his criticism, Venus smashes an urn [**Uranus**] over his head. "I would rather go fishing with **Neptune,**" she snarls "or take my dog **Pluto** for a walk than go out with you!" She leaves in a huff.

You must admit that a story like that is much easier to remember than the dry facts on their own!

Some people, however, find this rhyme difficult to remember. There are many other ways to learn and remember the same information; you have to find the mnemonic that works for you.

Another strong favorite for remembering the days of the months is shown below. Hold your fists out in front of you, side by side, and count from the left. The long months will fall on the knuckles, the short months in the hollows. Ignore your right pinkie when you use this trick.

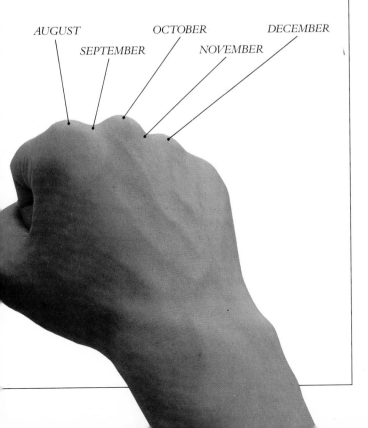

AUGUST   OCTOBER   DECEMBER
SEPTEMBER   NOVEMBER

wish to remember. If you have plans to meet a friend at a certain hour, for instance, you might compose the following lines of doggerel:

> Meeting John at eight.
> That's a fact, and I won't be late.

Because no other time of the day will rhyme with "late," there is no risk of becoming confused about the time of your appointment.

Acrostics and acronyms

An acrostic is a phrase or sentence constructed so that the initial letters of the words convey information or serve as cues. "He Often Mends Ellie's Socks," for example, provides the initial letters of the names of the five Great Lakes (Huron, Ontario, Michigan, Erie, and Superior). An acronym, on the other hand, uses a single word (HOMES, in this instance) made up purely of the initial letters to convey the same information.

In recent years acronyms have become extremely popular for the naming of action groups, government agencies, and companies. Although it is not always possible to find an acronym to fit gracefully, when they do work they are pleasingly economical and effective memory joggers.

Some acrostics have been handed down from one generation to the next. For example, countless children have learned to use the statement "**a r**at **in** the **h**ouse **m**ight **e**at **t**he **i**ce **c**ream" to help them with the spelling of "arithmetic." Acrostics can also be a boon to specialized fields of study. Medical students, for instance, commit to memory this couplet to help them remember the names of the 12 cranial nerves:

> On Old Olympus's Towering Top
> A Finn And German Vied At Hops.

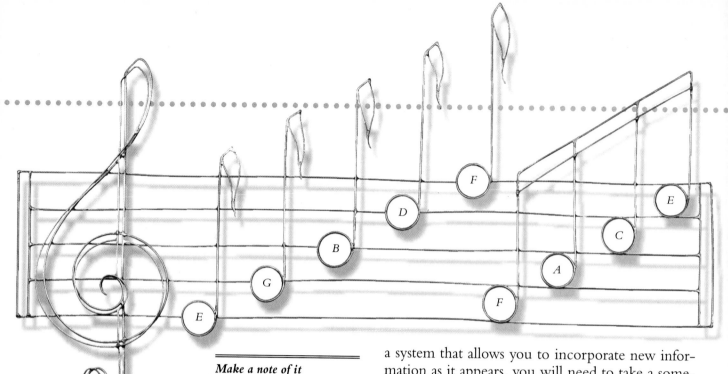

Each word is a cue to the name of a nerve: Optic, Olfactory, Oculomotor, Trochlear, Trigeminal, Abducens, Facial, Auditory, Glossopharyngeal, Vagus, Accessory, and Hypoglossal. Other specialist fields have their own favorite mnemonics.

Mnemonic systems

The memory aids described up to this point have all been short and relatively easy to remember. Each of them was created to help bring to mind a specific piece of information. For a system that allows you to incorporate new information as it appears, you will need to take a somewhat more complicated approach.

Some of the best and most effective mnemonic systems have been ones designed to help in remembering numbers. Many people remember phone numbers, for instance, by making use of the letters assigned to the various digits on the telephone. The number 843-2378 could be remembered as THE BEST, for example, while 255-3687 might be ALL FOUR.

Mnemonic systems that have uses which do not rely on such luck are necessarily somewhat more daunting. But once they are learned, their value is enormous. One such system involves assigning a consonant to each of the digits 0 through 9. The consonants are, in most cases, chosen for their resemblance to the digits for which they stand:

0 = z (for zero)
1 = t (one vertical stroke)
2 = n (two vertical strokes)
3 = m (three vertical strokes)
4 = r (the last letter of "four")
5 = l (five fingers with the thumb extended)
6 = b (b and 6 look alike)
7 = k (a mirrored 7 leaning against a line)
8 = d (in script, d has two loops)
9 = p (p backwards looks like 9)

By inserting vowels and allowing yourself to use the letter "s," you can use this truncated alphabet to form words that are easier to remember than the numbers they represent. For example, 31 could be MaT, and 536 becomes LaMB. The telephone number for the White House in Washington is currently 202 456-1414, which could be remembered as "No Zoo, No RuLes, BesT ReTiRe." For longer strings of digits, such as your Social Security number, or the number of your credit card, remember that you can divide these numbers any way that suits your purposes.

The fun factor

Mnemonics that are funny have particular value because—in many cases—you will remember best that which makes you laugh. Puns make people groan, precisely because they are so awful. But that very quality may render them more attractive as mnemonics. To remember the capital of Hungary, note that when you are hungry, your stomach is nothing "Bud-a-pest," and to remember that Ankara is the capital of Turkey, you could imagine a Thanksgiving turkey rendered immobile by a heavy weight, and her executioner rejoicing with the words, "Now that'll *anchor her* down!"

Obviously the more tricks you have for dealing with memory problems, the better your chances for quickly settling on something that will help you learn new information. The great value in making up your own mnemonics is that personal edge that you can give them. Do not hesitate to make your mnemonics ribald, or to make references to people, places, or subjects that amuse you. These are your memory aids, and only you can know what is going to serve you best.

SENSATIONAL SELL

Advertisers frequently use mnemonic devices such as rhyming slogans, repetition, and acronyms to make their products more memorable. Slogans such as "Thank heaven for 7-Eleven" stick in your mind because they rhyme, whereas the marketers of Doublemint gum are more likely to count on the repetition of the word "double" to imprint their product on the purchasing public's memory.

But ads must not only be memorable, they must prompt you to buy the product. If you remember the powerful image but not the name of the product, the advertiser has clearly failed. You can tell which advertisements have worked best on you by noting whether or not you can remember the key words or whether you find yourself humming the jingle. Successful ads may stick in your mind even when you don't want them to, because your memory can't escape things that are planted with an effective mnemonic.

VISUAL IMAGERY

IMAGINE A HORSE. Now imagine telling someone about that horse. Can you see it clearly in your mind? What color is it? Is its mane loose or braided? Is it carrying a saddle or wearing a bridle? Is it leaning out of a stable door or running free in a field of buttercups? How tall is it? If you stood next to it, could you put your hand on its back?

These questions are designed to sharpen your image of the horse. When first asked to imagine the animal, you probably had a vague notion of what it looked like. But once you started to pin down the details, your vision became clearer and livelier—and, as a consequence, much easier to remember. By getting in the habit of forming such vivid, detailed visual images in your mind, you can provide yourself with an invaluable memory tool.

Power of the imagination

Visual imagery can be powerful. In one study, a group of people asked to imagine they were walking down a familiar street and holding a cannonball took longer to accomplish the task than did a group asked to imagine doing the walk holding a balloon. The imagined weight of the cannonball they had visualized was so vivid that it actually slowed them down.

It has been conclusively proven that this power of visual imagery can be used to bolster the effectiveness of memory. As experiments have demonstrated, words for concrete objects, such as penguin, diamond, or airplane, are easier to remember than words for abstract ideas, such as manners, frequency, or possibility. This is because abstract ideas do not suggest a visual image. Similarly, it has been shown that when children are encouraged to visualize the stories they read, they remember far better than when they simply read the words. The more vivid you can make your visual imagery, the better your memory will be. Imaginative or unusual images are more memorable than common, everyday ones. A measure of colorful imagination can dress up your visual images. The three strategies that follow should help you give a memorable twist to your visual imagery.

A question of size
Keep forgetting your pen?
Imagine it as tall as a
skyscraper or so small it is
difficult to grasp. Such images
can be excellent memory aids.

First, try changing the scale of the things you want to remember. Enlarge a flea to human size in your mind's eye, or shrink an elephant to the size of a mouse. Give the object a context to measure the size against. Is it big enough to cast a shadow over the city? Small enough to fit in your hand? If, for instance, you want to remember to take your pen with you in the morning, think of it as a towering object, looming over the house as you walk out of the front door. There is a good chance you will recall this image as you set out for work.

A second approach is to revise your mental picture of the object's function or purpose. Reversing roles or changing them so that they seem bizarre can make ordinary ideas funny and memorable. To remember to walk a dog, picture the animal taking you out at the end of a leash. If you have to remember to write the camera manufacturer, think of your camera squirting ink. Try to get in the habit of challenging your usual perception of an object or the way a thing works.

Material change

A final strategy for spicing up your mental images is to picture the objects that you hope to remember made out of completely different materials. Imagine picking up a beach ball made from lead, or licking an ice-cream cone with the texture of sand. Changing the weight, feel, or construction of the object in your mind will help it stand out in memory.

Twisting images around in this way, or giving them bizarre qualities, will improve your memory for all sorts of things. If you have to call your dentist, think of him as a

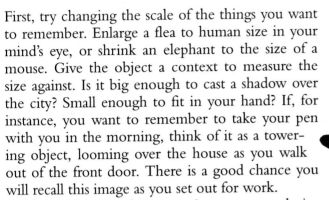

A full tank
To remind yourself to put gas in your car in the morning, create a visual image like this one that links the task to the time. The act of pouring milk on your breakfast cereal will then trigger your memory.

giant tooth, complete with mustache and glasses. Advertisers count on this technique when they show you bottles of mouthwash fighting off gingivitis with swords or when they depict powerful men emerging from a washing machine. By personifying the product in such offbeat ways, the advertisers hope to make a dent in your memory.

Because they are concrete and memorable in themselves, visual images can be used to remind you of almost anything. As memory triggers, they work best connected to a cue—something you are almost certain to see or do that will instantly bring the image to mind.

For instance, when John promised a work colleague that he would feed her cat while she was away on vacation, he was concerned that he might forget to stop by her house on his way home from the office—remembering to feed it while stuck in an afternoon meeting would be no good. Since John usually stopped for a drink after work, he fortified his memory by imagining a bottle on the bar sporting whiskers and a tail. This image served him well: As soon as he sat down at the bar, it triggered thoughts of his friend's pet.

You can also use visual imagery to remember new words, when studying a foreign language or simply expanding their English vocabulary. For example, when learning the French word *parler*, to speak, think of parsley for the sound, then reinforce the meaning by imagining two bunches of the green, leafy herb engaged in conversation. To recall the meaning of the English word *scurrilous*—coarse-mouthed, abusive, or vulgar—think of a squirrel (*squirrilous*) that watches you from atop a fence, chattering loudly and rudely. Such visual mnemonics can be wonderfully effective in rooting new words in your memory.

But visualization can have memory applications beyond the simple recalling of individual facts.

Tailoring your image

John's mental image of a furry, purring bottle served well in reminding him to feed his colleague's cat. It worked *because it made a link to his daily routine. Use this technique to remind yourself of any easily forgotten chore.*

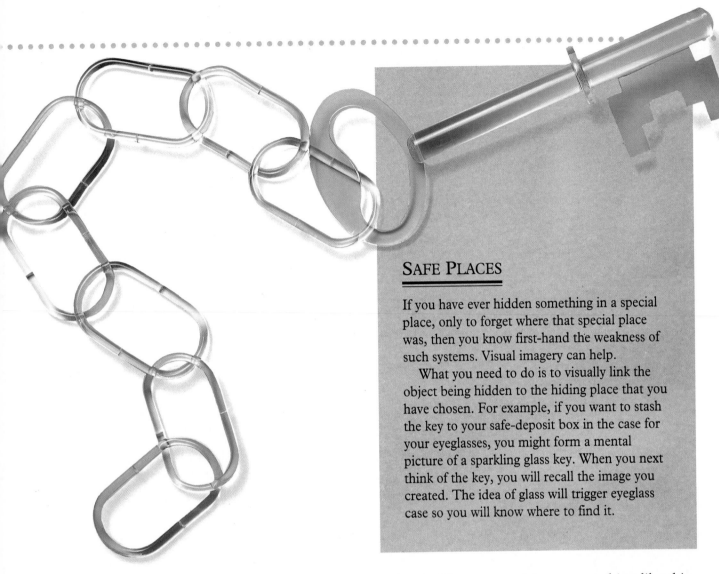

SAFE PLACES

If you have ever hidden something in a special place, only to forget where that special place was, then you know first-hand the weakness of such systems. Visual imagery can help.

What you need to do is to visually link the object being hidden to the hiding place that you have chosen. For example, if you want to stash the key to your safe-deposit box in the case for your eyeglasses, you might form a mental picture of a sparkling glass key. When you next think of the key, you will recall the image you created. The idea of glass will trigger eyeglass case so you will know where to find it.

Stringing images together into some form of apt and memorable narrative can help you to remember even fairly complicated packages of disparate information with relative ease.

To make your visual stories memorable, take the time to imagine your characters in detail, complete with height, weight, look, smell, and personality. Then have them interact. If, for instance, a dog bites a man in your memory drama, you may want to have the man burst out crying or bite the dog back. Whatever happens, it is important that the characters react to each other memorably.

Motoring memories

Say you are a law student trying to memorize the details of a legal case, including the participants' names and their roles in the case. A challenge has been raised to widow Cindy Carson's right to her deceased husband's estate. Carl Teitelbaum is the prosecutor, and Sanford White is Ms. Carson's

attorney. Your story might go something like this: *Cinderella* [Cindy] is driving her *car* toward the *sun* [Carson]. Heading straight for her is a lawyer with a *cruel* [Carl] face who tosses the *title* [Teitel] deeds of her estate out of his car before the vehicles collide with a resounding *boom* [baum, which combines with Teitel to produce Teitelbaum]. A *white Ford* in the background is seen reversing out of *sand* [Sanford White] to come to the rescue. The device of visualizing the car operating in reverse reminds you that the elements white, Ford, and sand must also be recalled in reverse.

Note that the relationships between the players in the drama should conform to their original roles and characteristics—so Teitelbaum, the prosecutor, must attack the widow, and White must defend her. In addition, bearing in mind that you will want to recall your own stories quickly, make sure that your images really mean something to you and are thus easily deciphered.

VISUALIZATION PRACTICE

Visualization techniques play a large part in improving your memory, and developing your ability to use them is therefore vital. These two pages will help you practice a basic visualization technique—creating imaginative visual combinations with two common objects. The images for each example progress in their complexity, showing the visualization process in action. It is quite common for people who use this technique regularly to follow such a progression—to think up two or three images of increasing complexity—before settling on one that really works.

Follow these examples, then turn the page to read about one of the most useful memory techniques you will ever learn, and one for which visualization skills are essential—the peg system.

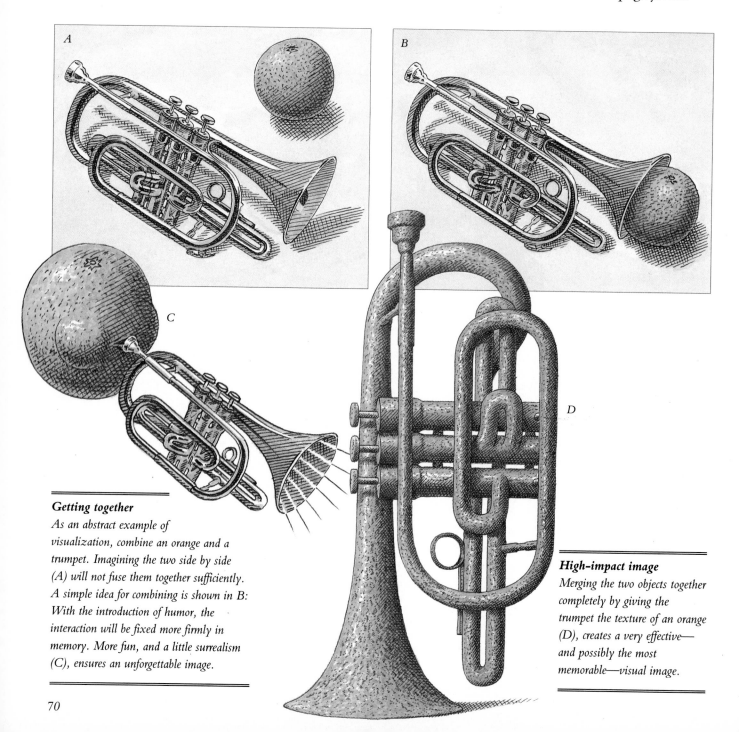

Getting together

As an abstract example of visualization, combine an orange and a trumpet. Imagining the two side by side (A) will not fuse them together sufficiently. A simple idea for combining is shown in B: With the introduction of humor, the interaction will be fixed more firmly in memory. More fun, and a little surrealism (C), ensures an unforgettable image.

High-impact image

Merging the two objects together completely by giving the trumpet the texture of an orange (D), creates a very effective—and possibly the most memorable—visual image.

A practical problem

Suppose you need to remember that you hid a present under the bed. You might visualize the bed on top of a room-size present (E). Or you might imagine the present covered in a bed-motif gift-wrap (F). Or wrap a huge bow around the bed (G).

Route to success

Imagine you are delivering a package to someone who lives on Crabtree Avenue. To remember the address, first marry the words "crab" and "tree." You could visualize a tree sprouting crabs on the end of its branches (H), or you could give the crab some leafy legs (I). Finally, place your chosen crab-tree image in context on an avenue (J).

HOOKS FOR MEMORY

Ten to remember
It is especially difficult to remember lists of unconnected objects, like these 10 things to be packed for a trip. One way is to "hook" the objects onto "peg" words that rhyme with the numbers one through 10.

One of the most widely known techniques for remembering large or difficult lists is the peg-word system. To use it, begin by selecting familiar words that will act as pegs on which to hang the information you wish to remember. Then, making use of association and visualization, link the new information to the peg words.

The most common group of peg words is one involving 10 names of concrete objects, all of which rhyme with a number from one to 10: One is bun, two is shoe, three is tree, four is door, five is hive, six is sticks, seven is heaven, eight is gate, nine is line, ten is hen. Because you know these numbers so well, you will have little difficulty remembering the peg words with which they are matched, and you will soon be ready to use them to master more complicated information.

For example, if you wanted to memorize the objects in the illustration above, you would run through the list, making visual associations between the peg words and the items to be learned. You might associate the camera with the bun (one) by picturing a man holding a bun to his eye and squeezing an imaginary shutter. You could associate the saucepan with the shoe (two), by imagining an old shoe simmering in a pan on the stove. Similarly, the teddy bear could be dangling from the branch of a tree (three), and so on.

Because this memory system relies on your ability to manipulate and recall your 10 peg words fluently, it is worth spending a little time deciding what yours will be and figuring out your visual images for each. The list above is only a suggestion; you might prefer six=tricks or eight=skate, for example. Whatever your choice, make sure you are happy with all your images.

Longer lists

For lists of more than 10 items, you will need to double back and use the peg words again and again, each time with a slight variation. When you reuse the peg words, give the list a different theme each time through. For items 11 through 20, for example, the theme could be sadness: The bun could be soggy, the shoe could have holes, the tree might be leafless, the door creaky, and so forth.

The peg-word system is especially useful for shopping lists, schedules, and historical facts which

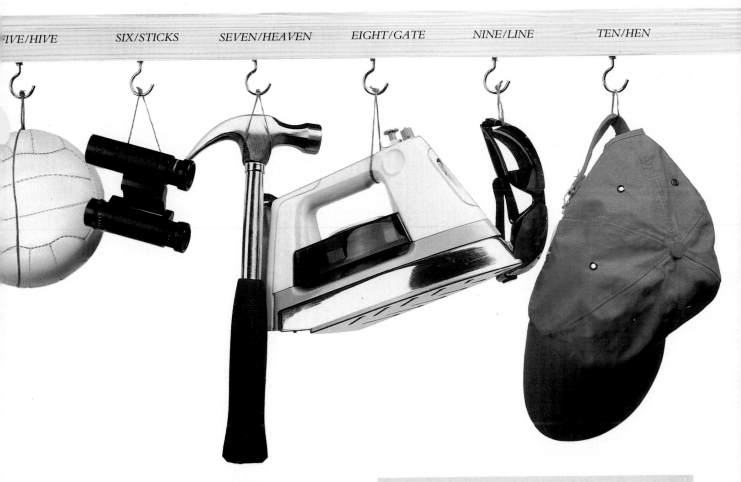

FIVE/HIVE   SIX/STICKS   SEVEN/HEAVEN   EIGHT/GATE   NINE/LINE   TEN/HEN

need to be remembered in order. On a grocery list, for example, you might have oranges, carrots, and potatoes, so you could visualize oranges squeezed over a bun, carrots sticking out of a shoe, potatoes sprouting from a tree, and so on.

But the peg-word system really shines when you need to memorize complicated lists. An example is the periodic table of elements and their atomic numbers: hydrogen (1), helium (2), lithium (3), beryllium (4), boron (5), carbon (6), nitrogen (7), oxygen (8), fluorine (9), and neon (10). Use your association skills first to connect each element with a concrete word that reminds you of its name—perhaps "hide" for hydrogen, "heel" for helium, "lithe" for lithium, "bell" for beryllium, and so forth. You then link each one to your peg words: Hide with bun, heel with shoe, lithe with tree, and so on. Thus with good visualization and association skills, you can use the peg-word system to memorize any list, however complex.

ADAPTING YOUR TECHNIQUE

This version of the peg-word system relies on words that rhyme with numbers. An equally effective system could be based on visual puns, with the peg words resembling the numbers to which they correspond: One could be a post, two a swan, three could be lips, and so on. You could then use your imagination to link this new assortment of peg words to the things that you need to remember. Say that you have decided to make four a ballerina, and that your fourth chore of the afternoon is to pick up the dry cleaning. You might imagine your ballerina dancing across the stage wearing the raincoat you left at the cleaners. This unusual image will probably stick in your mind pretty well.

MEMORY PLACES

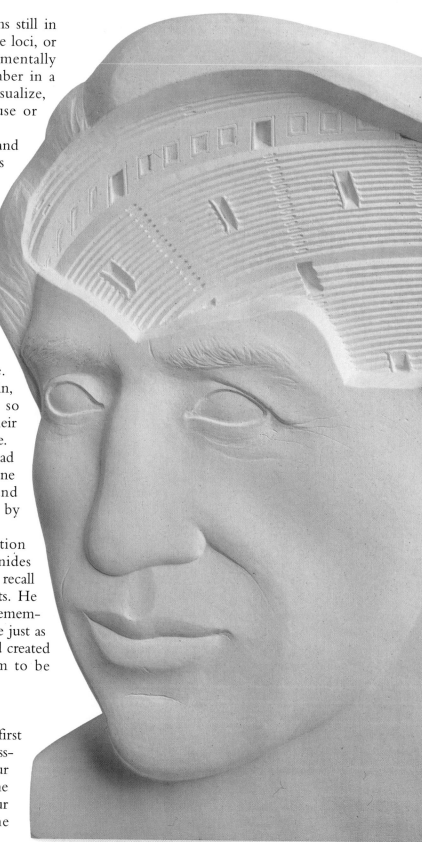

ONE OF THE OLDEST memory systems still in use today is called the method of the loci, or places. This mnemonic trick involves mentally placing the objects you want to remember in a familiar location that you can easily visualize, such as around the rooms of your house or along a neighborhood street.

Like the peg-word system (pages 72 and 73), the method of the loci at first seems somewhat contrived and complex. Yet centuries of use have proved it effective for remembering large amounts of disparate information, such as lists of unrelated items or tasks.

The perfect place

Legend has it that some 2,500 years ago, the Greek poet Simonides was invited to address a great banquet held in honor of an Olympic athlete. The poet delivered his eulogy and left the table. Minutes later, the roof of the hall caved in, killing most of the guests. Many were so badly mutilated that—to the distress of their relatives—they were no longer recognizable.

It then dawned on Simonides that he had a complete mental picture of where everyone had been seated during the banquet and could identify the bodies of the dead by recalling their positions.

Suspecting that this kind of visualization could be applied more generally, Simonides later tried substituting items he wanted to recall for each of the remembered dinner guests. He found that he could virtually "see" the remembered items ranged around the dinner table just as he had "seen" the deceased guests. He had created a memory system that linked each item to be remembered with a specific place.

Doing it yourself

To use Simonides' technique, you must first choose a location you can visualize effortlessly and in detail. It can be any place—your home, your office, a familiar street, a scene from a painting you remember, or even your own body. This location will anchor the whole system, so you must know it well.

Theater of the mind

To enhance his memory, 16th-century Italian scholar Giulio Camillo used to imagine himself standing on the stage in an amphitheater, looking up at its 49 blocks of seats. In each block he would mentally place up to six items that he wished to remember. By visualizing the various sections of the amphitheater, Camillo could then effectively recall nearly 300 objects.

You are now ready to remember a list of tasks for the day. Say you have to pay a bill, get your hair cut, reserve a table at a Greek restaurant, and call your mother. Using the principles set forth in "Visual imagery" (pages 66 to 73), create a vivid image that represents each task. Then place them mentally in your location. If it is a park, for instance, you might visualize the bill as a paper boat on a lake, and a hair cut as a bush being pruned by a gardener into the shape of a hair brush. A player on the softball diamond using a kabob for a bat could remind you to reserve that Greek restaurant table, and your mother playing with a giant telephone in the sandbox will remind you to call her.

A STREETWISE RUSSIAN

Imagine what you would see if you flew low over your home town or district, with its buildings, streets, and people spread out below you. Solomon Shereshevskii, a Russian memory expert in the 1920s, used this mental image in a very effective mnemonic device that you, too, can learn to employ.

When he wanted to remember a list of names, Shereshevskii would form a visual image for each of the names and then mentally place them along a Moscow street he knew well. To recall the list, he imagined himself flying above the street, viewing the images as they passed below him—one in a shop doorway, another against a lamppost, a third outside a café. Using this memory technique, he could even remember addresses and telephone numbers without ever having to make a note.

If you want to try this system yourself, you will need to focus on a street that is very familiar and start with a short list of things to be remembered. Once you have practiced the technique with these simple lists, you can progress to more complex memory challenges.

It is important to establish a set number of loci at the outset and to proceed through them in a fixed sequence. This will insure against overlooking items and enable you to recall them in order. Using your body as the anchor location to remember 10 items, for instance, you would travel from top down: Top of your head, mouth, neck, shoulders, chest, stomach, hips, hands, knees, and feet.

You will find that it is possible—perhaps even helpful—to use the same anchor location over and over, but it is also advisable to have several anchor locations to fall back on when using this memory system. In this way you will be able to memorize longer lists of items. The first 10 items of any list, for example, could be placed mentally in a park location and the next 10 in a favorite painting.

As with other memory aids, the loci system works best when the items themselves are unusual or appear in unexpected places. You won't remember to buy an extra quart of milk, for instance, if you imagine milk in the refrigerator. Such a mundane image can easily slip from your memory. Visualizing a cow sitting on a chair in the hall waiting to be milked would be a better bet.

Developing your technique

Now, exercise your newfound skills. Imagine that you need to remember to write to your grandmother, clean your car, make an appointment with your doctor, and buy some food for your dog. First create a visual image for each task—an old-fashioned quill pen, for example, might remind you to write the letter to your grandmother—and then mentally place each one in your anchor location.

Visualizing and placing these four tasks should

Body memory
The body offers a convenient location for recalling any type of information. Suppose, for instance, you were a biology student who wanted to memorize the vertebrate families—fish, amphibians, reptiles, birds, and mammals—in evolutionary order. You could imagine a fish on your hat, a frog popping out of your mouth, a snake curled round your neck, wings growing from your shoulders, and a baby kangaroo nestling on your chest.

Personal favorites

You can use a mental image of your favorite painting as a location for memory reminders.

American Gothic *by Grant Wood offers possibilities for memorizing a shopping list.*

take about two minutes. Mark the time when you finished fixing these items in your memory and then carry on reading. After about half an hour, think again of your anchor location. You should find that the four tasks are fresh in your memory and visible to your mind's eye. They will probably be just as easy to recall the day after you try this exercise. With practice, you will be able to remember longer lists of items in this way.

Abstract images

The loci system works well with lists of tasks and objects that you wish to remember, but things such as names and numbers pose special problems. Using techniques such as association you must first turn names and numbers into more concrete visual images. (See "Remembering names" on pages 84 to 91 and "A head for figures" on pages 92 to 99.) Once you have done so, this memory system will generally yield good results. You may even find that the loci method's real strength is in helping you remember abstractions.

Like any other complex mnemonic system, the loci method must be practiced a good while before it begins to seem natural. But if you take the trouble to master this approach, you will be amazed at how well it will serve you as a memory aid.

A SPECIAL CALENDAR

Although the traditional method of the loci uses places to help you remember things, you can make comparable use of any system of ideas.

For example, if you are a devotee of astrology and remember perfectly the order in which the 12 signs of the zodiac occur, you can use them to anchor a list of 12 items in your memory. You might mentally turn the water spilling from Aquarius's urn into parcels to remind yourself to buy a birthday present for your nephew. Similarly, you could imagine the fish of Pisces swimming inside a washing machine to remind yourself to start the laundry, and then visualize the ram of Aries driving your car as a reminder that your car needs servicing.

NO PLACE LIKE HOME

When applying the method of the loci, do not overlook the advantages of using your home as an anchor location in which to mentally position the things you need to remember. For most people using this technique, it is easy to visualize a walking tour through their homes because they have made such tours so many times before.

If the method is to work to full effect, it is best to plot the same course each time you memorize a list. For the home illustrated below, the sequence moves from the middle of the stairs to the clock in the hall, on to the fireplace mantel, to the armchair in the living room, to the stove, and last, to the kitchen floor. Any subsequent memory lists would follow the same route around the house. As you become increasingly familiar with the positions you have chosen, you will memorize lists more quickly and recall the items more confidently.

Another way to better your chances of success with this technique is to dream up mental images that are as unusual or amusing as possible. Place these items where you would least expect to find them. In the example below, the giant false teeth that replace the kitchen table are a memorable reminder for anything to do with dental care. Likewise, the old-fashioned telephone, out of place on the stove-top, is an image likely to linger for some time.

Fantasy tour

In the image of the home below, objects have been placed to serve as reminders for different tasks. Mentally walking through the rooms, you would be reminded to buy a birthday present for your sister, respond to a party invitation, return a library book, take your coat to be cleaned, make an important phone call, and go to the dentist.

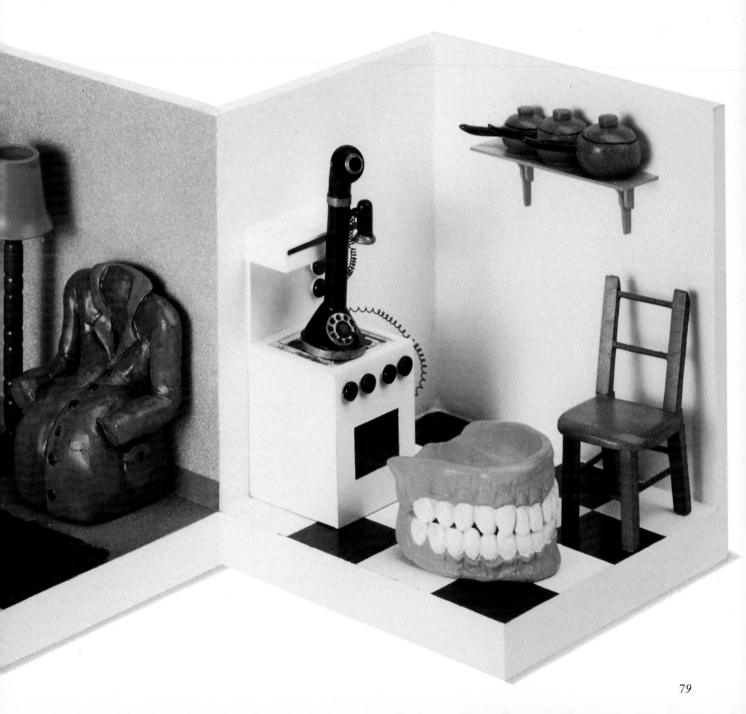

REMEMBERING FACES

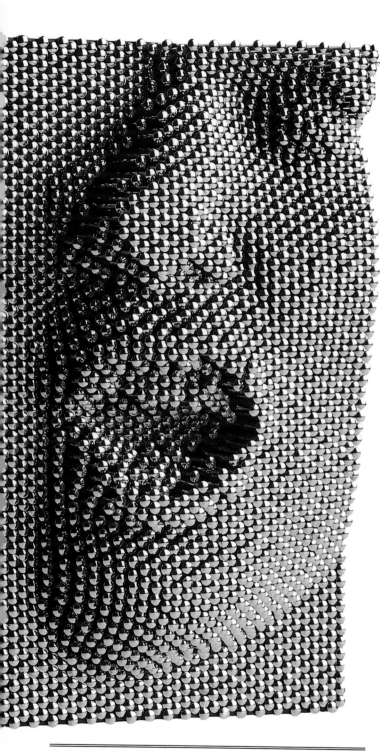

Facial impressions

The ability to remember and recognize faces varies from person to person. Research has shown that children and old people tend to have the worst *memories for faces. Strangely, though women seem to remember faces better than men, it is the faces of other women they recall best.*

YOU ARE AT A PARTY. A man comes over and greets you warmly. He calls you by name and clearly expects you to recognize him. But you are mystified—not only have you forgotten his name, you have no recollection of having met him before.

People dread this scenario of social embarrassment. It is embarrassing enough to forget a name, but if you can't remember the face either, there is little chance you will ever remember anything about this person without a prompt.

For some people, failure to recognize faces is a daily torment. They live in perpetual fear of committing social gaffes, peer anxiously at complete strangers, and pass old friends by on the street. In extreme cases, the problem is brought on by a neurological condition called prosopagnosia. People afflicted with this condition can identify familiar furniture and clothing but fail to recognize even their closest family. Everyone forgets a face from time to time, but such extreme memory loss is rare.

A good memory for faces can be a great help when recalling people in their absence. A teacher asked to write a reference for a former student, for instance, must visualize just what distinguished that student from the rest of the class. If the teacher cannot conjure up a picture of the student's face, the reference will be uninspired (or even impossible to do). This is because facts and feelings tend to cluster around the memory of a person's appearance. You are unlikely to recall much about a person whose face you cannot remember.

Take another look

If you forget a face, it is highly probable that you did not look at it closely. To overcome this problem, inspect everyone you meet with care; try to fix the features of each new face in your mind. It may seem excessive to go to this trouble, but there are two good reasons for doing so. First of all, you cannot tell whose face you may want to recall at a later date. But even more important, your memory for faces will benefit from the practice.

Scan each person's face with deliberate interest. Take particular note of the details that make the face unique—a patch of pitted skin, a slightly bulbous nose, or an unusually square chin. This conscious effort to observe people well will greatly enhance your ability to recognize their faces later.

FACIAL INVERSION

Can you recognize these famous faces without turning the page upside down? (Solutions on page 140.)

This simple test was probably harder than you thought. Researchers have come to the surprising conclusion that it is more difficult to recognize upside-down faces than to do the same for inverted buildings or other objects that have been turned on their head. The reason may lie in the fact that the brain has a specific mechanism for analyzing facial features separately from all other visual information.

Inverting the face throws this face-recognition mechanism out of whack, leaving you to struggle with the problem as if you had little practical experience at recognizing faces.

If you had difficulty completing this exercise correctly, you will have some idea of the problems encountered daily by people whose ability to recognize faces is impaired.

Once you start examining faces more carefully, you will need to find ways to plant these observations firmly in your memory. One method is to exaggerate the most notable elements of the face in your mind. Pick out details that you find distinctive—a large nose, a dimple in the chin, ears that stick out, a mole high on the cheekbone, almond-shaped eyes—and visualize an exaggerated or distorted version of those features until you have a caricature that amuses you.

Alternatively, you might focus on a more abstract quality of the face. Is it kind, happy, intelligent or sour? Is the person's expression deadpan or animated? For this exercise, call upon your powers of association. If the face looks motherly, imagine a host of small children climbing around your subject. If the face is lined and tan, imagine the person sailing, hair flowing in the wind. When called upon to remember the faces later, your association should serve you well as a reminder.

Verbal description

Describing a face in words can also be a help in remembering it. To describe a face adequately to yourself, you will have to look it over pretty thoroughly. To create a complete verbal description, take in the subject's general appearance. Decide whether the head is small or large in relation to the

Imaginary golfer

Mental imagery can be used to reinforce your memory of a face. One strategy is to imagine the person doing something that fits his or her face. For example, if a man has a suntan and a sporty look, you might picture him outdoors playing golf.

body, and whether it is heart-shaped, oval, round, or square. Next describe each feature individually and build a detailed picture in your mind. Finally, add distinguishing features, such as an unusual hairdo, dimples, or freckles. The face should then be indelibly fixed in your mind.

Although they can be powerful memory aids, words are crude substitutes for visual images.

Verbal description of the face will never take the place of the visual image in your mind. You may not be able to describe how you can distinguish one face from another, yet your eyes take in myriad details instantaneously and can detect even the most subtle of differences between faces. Once you have fixed a face in your mind, you will be able to recognize it for many years to come.

POINTS TO PONDER

Most people would have trouble identifying a friend from a picture of the person's eyes or nose—unless that particular feature was especially remarkable in some way. The difficulty stems from the fact that you remember faces as complete images, not as the sum of component features. You may be able to

improve your memory for faces, however, by purposely focusing on the details. In this technique, it is the effort you make studying a face that helps place it firmly in your memory. To give yourself some practice, examine the face of one of your friends and describe its features in detail.

Eyes and eyebrows

Note your first impressions of the eyes. Do they seem generally warm, kind, calm, alert, or cruel? Are they close together or far apart? Note their size and shape. Are they almond-shaped or round, wide or narrow? Examine the color of the eyes. Are they smoky gray or deep blue? Are the eyebrows thick and bushy or thin and arched?

Ears

The ears are not always visible if a person has long hair, but they are as individual as fingerprints. First note if they are set high or low on the head. They may lie flat or stick out prominently. Are they small with few contours or large with many folds? Are the lobes large or small? Check to see whether the lobes have been pierced.

Nose

Take a good look at the person's nose. Is it long or short? Does it dominate the face or fit in perfectly with the other features? Do the nostrils flare, making the nose look wider? Perhaps they are pinched, giving it a thin appearance. Are the nostrils hairy? Check for an upward or downward curve at the end, and notice how the nose looks in profile. Is it hooked, round, or pointed?

Mouth

The mouth is very expressive—make a note of the mood it conveys most often. Does the person smile frequently or do the lips naturally turn downward producing a sad expression? Is the mouth wide or narrow? Are the lips notably thin or particularly thick and full? Is one lip larger or more prominent than the other? Does the person have particularly white teeth—or unusually large gaps between the front teeth?

TEST YOUR MEMORY FOR FACES

Take a few seconds to study the face of the imaginary golfer on page 81. Then turn back to this page and, from memory, make up a picture of his face by selecting the proper eyes, ears, nose, and mouth from the options below. After making a note of your choices, turn back and study the face again, this time for several minutes. Observe the features one by one, then try the test again, noting a second list of choices. Did your performance improve? The solution is on page 140.

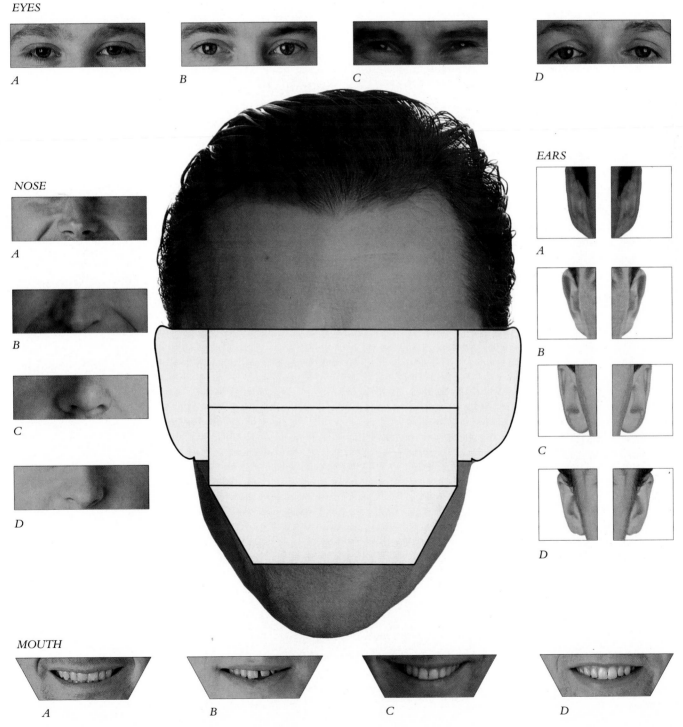

EYES

A B C D

NOSE

A

B

C

D

EARS

A

B

C

D

MOUTH

A B C D

REMEMBERING NAMES

ONCE YOU HAVE RECOGNIZED a face, you will probably begin to recall facts about that person such as where you first met and what he or she does for a living. The information you are least likely to recall is the person's name.

LINKING NAMES AND FACES

Although all parts of the brain are linked, the memory of how a face looks (visual material) is stored in the right hemisphere, while the name that goes with the face (verbal material) is stored in the left hemisphere. This is one reason why it is often difficult to put a name to a face.

One simple technique you can employ to alleviate this difficulty is to associate both the name and the face with some other aspect of the person, such as a hobby or an occupation. If, for example, you meet a doctor called Snow, imagine him with bushy white eyebrows above his surgical mask, and think of him standing at an operating table, set in a winter landscape.

As you probably found when trying the test on page 14, a name is a hard thing to remember. This may be because people's names are unrelated to their appearance. Janes do not look like Janes, Smiths do not look like Smiths. The arbitrary nature of names means that they are like words in a foreign language; a real effort is required to learn them. But the ability to remember names is a valuable social skill. Consider how hurt you feel when someone fails to remember your name.

Making the effort
In many cases, people aren't actually forgetting the names, they are simply failing to make the effort to learn them in the first place. How often have you offered excuses in advance by saying, "I've got a terrible memory for names?" Yet if a man offered you $1,000 to remember that his name was Michael Schwartz, you would almost certainly remember it. If you want to learn a name, first you must consciously decide to do so.

The next step is to be sure that you have heard the name properly; if you haven't heard it correctly, you cannot possibly expect to remember it. The same applies if you are distracted or preoccupied with other thoughts during the introduction. If you are ill at ease or worried about the impression you are creating, all your

NAME

INFORMATION

FACE

The triple jump
When you see a person you recognize, you are more likely to remember his occupation than his name. But remembering other details about his life can help you forge the link that will call the elusive name to mind.

OVERCOMING NAME BLOCKS

You may find that you are sometimes unable to remember the name of someone you know well. You are unlikely to have forgotten the name completely, yet you cannot recall it right away. To overcome a name block, try to remember as many facts about the person as possible. What does he do for a living? When did you last see him? Where does he live? The answers to these questions may provide vital clues that will jog your memory.

Sometimes a name you cannot recall simply pops into your memory later. This occurs either because the brain continues subconsciously to search for it while you are not thinking about it or because a final clue bridges the gap between the facts you remember about the person and the person's name.

Roll over Bert Haven

Trying to remember the name of a famous composer, you might recall that it begins with a "b." Listing possible names, however absurd, you may stumble on something close enough to jog your memory.

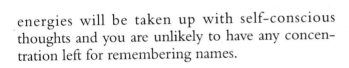

energies will be taken up with self-conscious thoughts and you are unlikely to have any concentration left for remembering names.

Paying attention

When you meet new people, look at them and listen carefully to their names. Do not hesitate to ask how difficult names are spelled or pronounced. Then in the first few minutes of conversation, repeat new names as often as you can do gracefully, to reinforce what you have learned.

Do not worry too much if this seems awkward. People enjoy being addressed by name and will think you are polite. If, for instance, you are introduced to someone named Peggy, you might say: "Hello, Peggy. Is that short for Margaret?" You could also link her name with that of another person you know: "There was a Peggy in my high school graduating class, and she had red hair, too!" Begin questions to your new acquaintance with her name: "So Peggy, do you live in the neighborhood?" And refer to her by name when talking to a third person: "Peggy tells me she lives just around the corner." Finally, when you part, acknowledge your conversation partner—whom you will now be expected to know when you meet again—by

addressing her by name for the last time: "I'm sorry I have to leave so soon. It was delightful meeting you today, Peggy."

This technique works well when you are introduced to one person at a time. In a group you may not be able to focus on each name quite so carefully. If you forget a name, don't be embarrassed to ask about it again later. Trying to get names right and making a point of remembering them flatters people and can only do you credit.

Forging the link

Before you can remember a person's name, you must first fix his or her face in your memory (see pages 80 to 83). Once you have studied the face and know it well, you must link it in your memory with the name. As with any other memory challenge, the key is to build meaningful links—or bridges—between unrelated bits of information.

Does the name fit the face in any obvious way? Does he really look like a Harold Hardy? If not, ask yourself why not. Is it perhaps because he looks kind and thoughtful rather than tough and "hard" as his family name suggests? If he looks happy you might fall back on a little alliteration—Happy Harry Hardy. Compare the person's face with that

Completing the Picture

It is much easier to remember biographical facts—what people do for a living, where they live, what hobbies they pursue—than it is to remember names, particularly with people you have met only recently. In devising visual images to help you hang onto the names, you can make things easier for yourself by incorporating biographical data. The more time and effort you spend working out an imaginative and colorful image, the stronger the image will be, and the more likely you will be to remember it.

Creating a vivid image
Mr. Baker is a writer who likes nothing better than to drive down to the ocean and go snorkeling in his spare time. To remember his name, imagine him in a baker's apron, working on a typewriter made out of bread. Add fish and a snorkel to the image, and you will remember not only his name but also everything else you know about him.

of other men you know, or with those of famous people with the same or a similar name. Do they share features in common that could serve as an effective hook in your memory?

Adding information
Where you cannot find a direct link between the face and the name you will need to find out more information about the person. By asking where people live, what work they do, or where they took their last vacation, you not only learn more about them and get to know them better, but also provide yourself with practical bits of information that you can use as hooks for recalling their names.

If, for instance, a woman called Rhoda tells you that she prefers to wear pants rather than skirts, you might see her as "Rode a [horse]" and imagine her in riding breeches. Or if you meet a man named Chuck who follows professional ice hockey, he could be "Chuck the puck." Once again, the more ridiculous the image is, the better it will function as a mnemonic device.

It is easiest to remember names that are familiar from other sources—brand names of commercial products, or the names of famous people. You can always, for instance, picture Ms. Ford driving around in a tiny Ford Fiesta or your new business acquaintance Mr. Reagan sitting in the Oval Office being interviewed by a pack of newspaper reporters.

Since most names conjure up no recognizable—and therefore memorable—associations, you will often have to create them yourself. One way to remember a difficult name is to find rhyming words that bring to mind concrete visual images. With the name Carruthers, for instance, you might see a "car with udders." If you go on to imagine Mr. Carruthers driving such a car, the sight of him will automatically trigger the memory of his name.

This technique works particularly well with unusual names of multiple syllables, which people frequently—and often unconsciously—transform into more familiar sounding phrases. A certain Professor Stetkevych, for instance, once called for a taxi and then reported his surprise at being greeted by the driver as "Professor Stuffed Cabbage." The Russian author Vlamidir Woinovitch had a similar experience. He was in a shop in New York having a manuscript photocopied and he was flattered to be recognized and called by name. But then he realized the man behind the counter was asking "One of each?" rather than "Woinovitch." You can deliberately transform complicated names in this way to make them more memorable. Because of

▶ PAGE 90

Memorable names
Names in fiction are most memorable when they reflect a character's nature. In his books, Charles Dickens named two teachers Mr. Gradgrind and Mr. Wackford Squeers, underscoring their harshness as disciplinarians. You will remember names better if you can establish similar links between people and their distinguishing characteristics.

PRACTICE MAKES PERFECT

Using imagery to help you remember names in everyday situations takes practice and imagination. Look at the names below and think of ways you could use images to remember them. Sometimes the name instantly suggests an image, other times you will have to break up the name into its syllables and substitute words with similar sounds to conjure up your image. The suggestions supplied may bring other possibilities to mind and help you to develop your own technique for creating images.

Mr. Fairbanks
Imagine him with fair hair, perhaps even a blonde wig, carrying large wads of money or holding up a bank.

Ms. Anderson
Break the name down into its syllables—"and-her-son." Then imagine a woman dragging her son with her everywhere.

Mr. Greenbaum
Picture him carrying a green bomb.

Ms. Zienkiewicz
Breaking this name down into syllables produces "zinc-with-itch." You could then picture her itching because of an allergy to zinc.

Mrs. Lissner
Mrs. Lissner could be a good listener. You could imagine her with very large ears.

Mr. Husayko
Break the name down into syllables that sound like the name—"who-says-so." You could then imagine him having an argument with someone.

Mrs. Shubat
Mrs. "Shoe-bat" sounds the same as Mrs. Shubat. Imagine her wearing oversized shoes and carrying a baseball bat.

Mr. Heiman
You could imagine Mr. "High-man" as a circus artist performing a skilled and dangerous act on the tightrope.

THE NAME GAME

Here is a chance to try out the techniques suggested in this section of the book. Imagine that you are with your fellow students at a reception marking the first night of a weekend course. The course organizer introduces you, saying with a laugh, "You probably won't remember all these names." See if you can prove him wrong. Study the faces and names on these two pages for about five minutes. Use your imagination and visual imagery skills to create links between the faces and the names. Then turn to page 91 and see if you can match the correct names to the various faces.

MR. MEHMET

MS. DINARD

MR. BLITZ

MS. APPLEBY

MRS. SORENSON

MS. NANDA

MS. LARKINS

MR. O'LEARY

MR. VAN DER MEER

MS. KUZAK

MR. SIKORSKI

MRS. PHILLIPS

TOO CLOSE FOR COMFORT

People sometimes find they are unable to remember names they ought to know well, and psychologists believe that there are, in many cases, important reasons for these lapses. In some instances, names remind people of events or feelings that are too painful to remember. Below are two examples of how the mind can block out names from memory.

The story of Ruth

Ruth worked in a large office and wanted to establish good relationships with the people around her. Yet she could only remember the names of her female colleagues. As hard as she tried, she always stumbled when it came to addressing the men.

Realizing she had a problem, Ruth enrolled in counseling. After approaching the problem in several ways without success, the counselor asked her to imagine walking down the hall of the office, greeting each man in turn. When asked how she felt, she admitted to a surprising degree of shame and embarrassment.

Further exploration revealed that Ruth was a deeply religious woman with a powerfully held belief that it was sinful for her to have warm feelings toward any man except her husband. The counselor pointed out that such feelings are common and do not represent any form of betrayal. Shortly thereafter, she was able to remember the names of all her colleagues, the men as well as the women.

Painful memories
Sigmund Freud, the founder of psychoanalysis, told of a man who was jilted by his fiancée. The man was devastated, and found he could not remember the name of the man she had married, even though he had known him for years. Freud believed that this patient had blocked out the husband's name because it reminded him of the pain he had felt when his fiancée had left him.

◄ PAGE 87

the special attention these unusual names require from the first, they generally stick in the mind far longer. Simple names, such as Smith or Jones, do not pique the imagination and are, perversely, much harder to remember.

Building standard images

To remember common names you will need your own set of standard images for each. When you meet someone named Smith, for example, you might imagine him or her hammering at a blacksmith's anvil. You might see a cone for Cohen, a beer glass for Stein, and an iceberg for Berg. With further information about the person you can then add the personal touch that will link the name to the particular individual. If you find out that Mr. Smith, for instance, is a teacher, you might imagine him hammering energetically on an anvil in front of a roomful of silent students.

Putting it all together

Since the memories for names and faces are stored in two different areas of the brain, you may need additional facts about the person to reinforce the image that links them together. Say that you find out Mr. Bannerman, whose name you are trying to remember, is a nurse and that he also plays in a rock-and-roll band during his off hours. Since Bannerman makes you think of "banana man," you might first visualize him as a banana. Increase the size of the banana in your mind to make it more memorable and then add whatever else you know about him. In the end, your mental image might be a giant banana wearing a lab coat and holding an electric guitar. This is a thought so bizarre that you will almost certainly be able to make the leap from Mr. Bannerman's face to his name the next time you see him.

In all of the examples presented thus far, you have been asked to devise an imaginative link between a name and a person. Despite its seeming complexity, visualizing images for the sake of remembering names forces you to pay close attention to the name and to expend a certain amount of mental effort inventing the precise memory image. This type of mental exercise keeps your thinking processes sharp and can only have a beneficial effect on your memory.

NAME CHECK

These are the 12 people you met on pages 88 and 89.
Imagine you are meeting them again the next day. Try
putting into practice the techniques for remembering names.
After you have identified as many of the people as you can,
turn to page 140 to see how well you did.

3 _____

1 _____

2 _____

4 _____

5 _____

8 _____

7 _____

6 _____

9 _____

10 _____

11 _____

12 _____

A HEAD FOR FIGURES

OST PEOPLE DO NOT even try to memorize numbers. If they need to remember a phone or bank ID number, they will generally write it down—and there is no question this is a sensible thing to do. But constantly having to look numbers up can be inconvenient. How often have you left your address book at home, forgotten where you wrote down the date of a friend's birthday, or not been able to find your social security number? Having important numbers instantly available in your head may seem difficult or even impossible to achieve, but is an enormously useful skill. And even a person who habitually panics when confronted with a row of figures can learn to remember numbers with a high degree of accuracy.

There are many different ways to memorize numbers, but most people rely on two main principles—association and visualization—with which you are now familiar. These are used in conjunction with the technique known as chunking, which can be a great aid to memory. Chunking involves breaking down long numbers into smaller "digestible" chunks. Nobody can memorize a long line of digits without chopping them up and seeing them, instead, as a series of shorter units.

Break it up
Look at the following numbers and read each one in turn. Do not study the numbers, just read them through digit by digit at a steady pace (about two digits per second). After reading each number, look away from the book or shut your eyes, and try to repeat it out loud.

538547	72385910
648372	854169375
3627294	4983287642

You probably found it close to impossible to recite the longer numbers accurately. Now try again with the same set of numbers, but this time read them in groups of two or three digits. Read them as larger numbers—"thirty-six," "twenty-seven," "two hundred and ninety-four," for example—

CHUNKING AND ASSOCIATION

Can you remember the following 16-digit number?
6313195730894510
Probably not. But you can if you break the number down into small chunks and make personal associations for each of them. Such a breakdown might include 63 (your mother's age), 13 (your daughter's age), 1957 (the year you started school), 30 (your waist measurement), 89 (August 9, your sister's birthday), 45 (the number of a friend's apartment), and 10 (your shoe size).

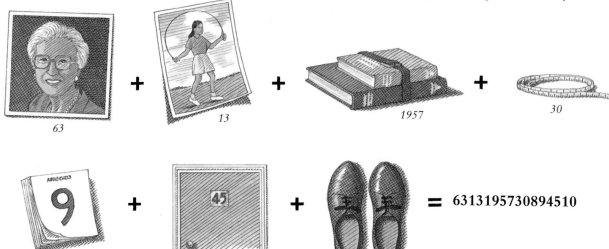

63 + 13 + 1957 + 30

89 + 45 + 10 = 6313195730894510

rather than as strings of individual digits. (Write the new, grouped, numbers down on a separate sheet of paper before you try the new test; 53 85 47, for example.) This time you will find it much easier to remember the sequences, and thus will see for yourself the value of chunking.

One effective number-memorizing technique depends on a combination of chunking and association: You split the number up into chunks and then give each of the chunks some personal association to fix it in memory.

At first blush, it may seem that you have few personal associations with numbers and so will have a difficult time using this method. But it is astonishing just how many associations most people can make if they try—everything from clothing sizes to dates, addresses, and ages.

The power of persistence

Applied persistently, this combination of chunking and association can be astonishingly effective. In an experiment conducted in 1982 (and later published in *The American Scientist*), a student who could initially recall no number longer than seven digits, gradually increased his skills until he was able to remember numbers more than 80 digits long.

The result was fascinating, but how did the student do it? It turned out that he was an enthusiastic amateur runner. As he read the numbers, he related them to running—"an excellent time for the 1,500 meters," or "two seconds less than my personal best." By chunking and associating the rows of numbers he was able to quickly store them away in his personal filing system, and to retrieve them easily.

You may not share this student's devotion to running, but just about any other special interest can provide the basis for number associations. You might be an enthusiastic golfer, for example, and relate numbers to your personal scores or to course records. If you follow pop music, you may call upon the dates of major recordings or references to numbers in songs. Or if you are an

Number confidence
Nowadays, a fear of dealing with numbers can be a serious handicap. Yet anyone can learn to memorize figures.

aficionado of fine automobiles you might associate numbers with everything from horsepower ratings of various engines to great model years. The theory is always the same: Split a large number up into chunks and relate them to whatever interests you.

Chunking stories

To ensure that the associations will stay in your memory for a long time—and that you will be able to recall the chunks in the right order—it sometimes helps to devise a little story. For the associations described in the box on page 92, for example, you might imagine your mother and daughter at your first school, tying a sash around your waist as

you prepare to go to your sister's birthday party. The celebration is to be held at a friend's apartment, which is a walkable distance away.

The story you create will be far more memorable if you make use of sensory impressions. Imagine, for example, the sound of your mother's voice as she talks to your daughter and your daughter's characteristic laughter. Think of the smells of floor polish and school lunches that will take you back to your school days. Picture the bright pink sash and remember the taste of the birthday cakes you ate in childhood. Think of the effort of climbing the many flights of stairs to your

Figuring it out

To remember a number like the diameter of the moon (2,160 miles) you might recall that your father's birthday is on 2/16 and that your bank balance is close to zero.

FASCINATING FACTS

Have you ever wished you could remember important dates, distances, and other figures for the sake of your general knowledge or simply to impress your friends? Using the methods you are learning in this book, you should be able to do just that.

Suppose you want to memorize the length of the Nile, which at 4,160 miles is one of the world's longest rivers. If you are a tennis fan, all you need to do is think of a doubles match taking place. You could imagine the river flowing down the middle of the court where the net should be. You then imagine the four players (4), using one ball (1). You know there is a minimum of six games in a set (6) and that nobody wants to score love (0). Try devising similar strategies to help yourself master four numbers that would be useful to have tucked away in memory. In a week's time, test yourself. You should find that you can remember them perfectly.

A hot number

The mean distance from the earth to the sun is 93,000,000 miles. You could picture this figure as the devil smoking a pipe (the 9) while holding a trident (with its 3 prongs) on which he is toasting six marshmallows (zeros—two to a prong).

friend's apartment. By imagining vivid details in this way, you stand a better chance of fixing the story, and thus the number, in your mind.

Pictorializing numbers

An alternative technique for memorizing numbers—particularly shorter ones—is known as pictorializing. To use this method, you first have to invent images for the digits from 0 to 9, possibly

Numbers into pictures

You can use these images for the numbers from 0 to 9 (or, of course, you can make up your own). Zero looks like an orange, 1 is like a rocket blasting off, 2 a swan, and 3 *the silhouette of a pregnant woman; 4 resembles a sailboat, 5 a ceiling hook, 6 a yo-yo, and 7 a boomerang; 8 could be a pair of glasses, and 9 a balloon on a stick.*

Getting the hang of it
The number 5 is shaped rather like a hook. To recall that the Plaza family lives in apartment 5, imagine them all being lifted by a crane.

sunglasses (8) while dangling from his finger (1), a colorful yo-yo (6). The more peculiar the image, the better you will remember it.

For longer numbers it may be necessary to construct a story instead of just an image, so that the order of the digits does not get lost. A story long enough to relate to a very long number, however, might begin to be too elaborate to commit to memory so you may want to combine pictorializing with chunking and association. To memorize the telephone number 334-5192, you might imagine a heavily pregnant woman (3) asking for your age (34) on May Day (5/1), then waving a large balloon (9) at a swan gliding by (2).

Whichever system or combination of systems you use, bear in mind that the more vividly you imprint the story or association in your mind, the more firmly you will plant the number in your memory. What often happens, of course, is that you gradually come to know the number automatically. But the beauty of learning it with a mnemonic technique is that the method would enable you to recall the number at will, should you find yourself with a mental block.

Another memory technique applicable to numbers is based on the conversion of digits into letters of the alphabet. This allows you to study words

connecting each number with an object that resembles it in shape. See page 95 for suggestions.

Once you have fixed in your mind 10 images for the digits 0 through 9, you can use them to remember short numbers very simply. To recall your padlock combination (0816), you could bring to mind a happy picture of the sun (0) wearing

Making a mind movie
You are in a multistory parking garage and have parked in space 12 on the fourth floor. To remember this location, you could construct the following movie sequence in your mind using the images on page 95. A sailboat (4) is gliding toward you. It lets off a rocket (1) that startles a swan (2), which flies away. This calls to mind the fourth floor and parking space 12.

rather than figures. A straightforward example of such a system, making use of similar characteristics between letters and numbers, was shown on page 64. A more complex variant was produced in England during the Victorian era by a Yorkshire headmaster known as the Reverend Brayshaw. He built a mnemonic system to help his pupils succeed in the rote-learning educational system of those times. Brayshaw devised rhymes for over 2,000 dates and other forms of numerical data in subjects ranging from history to physics. He used the following conversion system:

1	2	3	4	5	6	7	8	9	0	00
B	D	G	J	L	M	P	R	T	W	St
C	F	H	K		N	Q		V	X	
			S			Z				

With this formula, each date is converted to a set of consonants. You then insert vowels between the consonants to form a word. Hence the year Abraham Lincoln was assassinated, 1865, could be recorded as CRNL and read as CaRNaL. By working this word into a simple couplet, you can make the date of Lincoln's death entirely memorable: "CaRNaL thoughts are for Lincoln no more, Booth shot him, what a bore." Like all memory

TELEPHONE NUMBERS

Most seven-digit telephone numbers are written as groups of three and four digits. If you have particular difficulty remembering the four-digit part of phone numbers, try translating them into times on the 24-hour clock. For example, you could remember 1245 as "a quarter to one o'clock" and think of 2358 as "two minutes to midnight." Then conjure up images for those times of day. For the first example you could use the time made out of lunch food.

Another way to fix a telephone number in your mind is to think of a catchy phrase in which each word has the same number of letters as the number you are trying to remember. Using this system, 1665 might become "I desire dollar bills." Or you could recall the number for the local pizza delivery service with "Everyone loves those toppings on crispy pies" (855 8264).

Change of direction
Some people memorize phone numbers by finding patterns on the telephone keypad. Try to remember the number 741/258-9632, then look at the diagrams below and follow the arrows for a simple visual reminder.

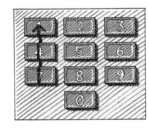 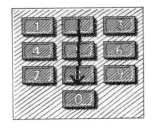

THE PI MAN

Most people would be pleased if they could improve their memory enough to be able to recollect telephone and credit card numbers without looking them up. But Rajan Mahadevan devotes his time to tasks such as learning the first 100,000 digits of pi. He has publicly recited as far as the 31,811th digit without a mistake. If you read out any five-digit sequence from the first 10,000 digits in this number, he can recite the next five.

Although scientists have proved that memory improves with practice, Rajan believes genetics are the root of his special gift: His father could recite all 154 of Shakespeare's sonnets, and his maternal grandfather had an instinct for numbers. He does, however, have his own peculiar systems. Rajan remembers the number 1745 better as 39, because Benjamin Franklin was born in 1706 and thus would have been 39 in 1745!

years 1981, 1941, 1964, and 1984, respectively. For example, President Ronald Reagan took office in 1981, Japan bombed Pearl Harbor in 1941, the Beatles first came to America in 1964, and the Olympics were held in Los Angeles in 1984. It does not even matter if the dates you are using are inaccurate—as long as you consistently associate them with the particular events.

One of the strengths of this particular memory trick is that you can use dates or other numbers as memory aids even if they are not exactly the same as the number you are trying to learn. You might, for instance, remember the number 57 because it is three years before the date of your birth (1960). If you are 30, you might remember the number 38 by thinking of it as your age in eight years time. Unlikely as this method may sound, it makes the number you are studying familiar and understandable. It will certainly give you good results.

A practical program

As with all areas of memory, you won't improve your ability to memorize numbers unless you make a concentrated effort. Set yourself the task of remembering all the numbers that you habitually use, rather than looking them up as you have in the past. Work systematically through your address book, learning each number in turn. Then get into the habit of routinely memorizing dates or figures that you come across when reading—the birthdays

systems, Brayshaw's mnemonic takes a certain amount of time and effort to learn. But once you have mastered the technique, it will enable you to remember large amounts of data in a fun way.

Dating technique

While some people need prompts to remember dates, others remember them so easily that they can use them to recall other number sequences. In trying to remember the social security number 081-41-6484, they might think of four events that happened in the

---

Using historical images
If you know the dates of the Civil War, 1861 to 1865, you can use them to remind you of other numbers. Say your baby-sitter's number is 6165, you could imagine her caught in the middle of the cross fire.

All wrapped up
To remember a sister's birthday on February 7, 1956 create a phrase like: "my (two letters) sister's (seven letters) never (five letters) grumpy (six letters)," or something equally suitable!

of film stars, for example, or world-record trivia. Your skill will improve gradually, and if you have the interest, you may go on to measure your memory against ever more difficult tasks, such as memorizing 20- or 30-digit numbers. This is unlikely to serve any practical purpose, of course, but if you are bitten by the memory bug, you may find it hard to resist. Remembering numbers with ease gives many people a sense of enhanced brain power and can lift your overall confidence level.

Number power
You might find inspiration in the achievements of great memorizers like Rajan Mahadevan (see box, opposite) and the late Professor A.C. Aitken of Edinburgh, Scotland, a numbers expert who lived from 1895 to 1967.

Aitken, like Mahadevan, dedicated considerable energy to learning the decimal places of pi. He found figures so interesting that he could not suppress his instinct for doing mathematical calculations. He saw 1961 not as, say, the year when Uri Gagarin made his pioneer flight into space, but as 37 times 53, and also 44 squared plus 5 squared, or even 40 squared plus 19 squared.

You are unlikely to achieve this level of comfort with figures, but you may be surprised at how memorable numbers can become.

NINES AT YOUR FINGERTIPS

Memorizing multiplication tables is a common task for children at school. But for the nine times table there is a simple technique for finding the answers. Spread out both hands. To calculate 2 x 9, bend the second finger of the left hand and count the fingers on either side of it— 1 to the left, 8 to the right. One next to 8 is 18.

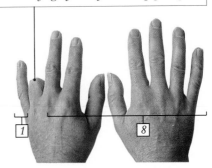

Bend second finger from left to multiply 2 by 9

2 x 9 = 18

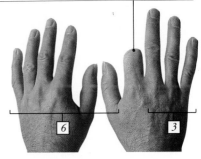

Bend seventh finger from left to multiply 7 by 9

7 x 9 = 63

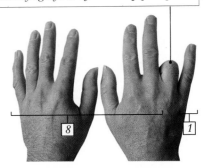

Bend ninth finger from left to multiply 9 by 9

9 x 9 = 81

Times nine
The finger trick works right through the nine times table. The fingers to the left of the bent one give the first figure of the answer, the fingers to the right give the second.

CHAPTER THREE

OVERCOME FORGETTING

IF SOMEONE OFFERED you a painless treatment that would prevent you from forgetting ever again, you would probably welcome it with open arms. After all, it would be wonderful to be able to recall all the figures that you need in business meetings and never again to be embarrassed at forgetting the birthdays of friends and relatives.

But a perfect memory would be a mixed blessing. Without the ability to forget, you would remember the hiccups your friend had as part of your conversation, and the sounds of papers being shuffled might take on the same weight as the information you acquired at a seminar.

Forgetting is, in fact, a useful aspect to memory. Information that is of no use has to be discarded. Those rare individuals with apparently perfect memories, such as the Russian journalist Solomon Shereshevskii, do not seem to do well academically and appear to have difficulty working out problems such as simple number progressions. Shereshevskii's extraordinary memory was only of use in allowing him to recall things exactly as he had heard or seen them.

If you had total recall, you would relive painful incidents with vivid clarity each time you thought about them. The natural process of forgetting allows unpleasant memories to recede with the passage of time. Indeed, research has shown that people can more easily recall pleasant memories than unpleasant ones. A good example of this might be the way in which mothers recall childbirth. The pain is quickly forgotten and the joy of the experience is recalled with clarity.

But in order to improve your memory, you need to regulate forgetting. Some things seem to be more forgettable than others, and understanding why this is so can help you begin to overcome memory problems. The first section of this chapter investigates the phenomenon of forgetting through time, the subtle ways in which details interfere with one another, and the effect of accidents or disease on memory. The second half of the chapter discusses the ways in which images of the past tend to gradually distort, producing a false memory full of subjective impressions and inaccuracies. It offers advice on what you can do to prevent this.

WHEN YOU REACH FOR INFORMATION IN YOUR MEMORY, YOU MAY OCCASIONALLY DRAW A BLANK. BY LIMITING THE BLANKS, YOU WILL IMPROVE YOUR HAND.

WHY DO WE FORGET?

"IF WE REMEMBERED everything, we should...be as ill as if we remembered nothing," wrote the 19th-century philosopher William James. Indeed, if the mind could not forget, it would soon become cluttered with useless trivia, making day-to-day decision-making extremely difficult.

The key to a good memory, of course, is the ability to retain important details while letting go of unimportant ones. But forgetting what you desperately want to remember is often difficult to avoid, as anyone who has studied for an examination or tried to memorize a long speech can attest.

Memory is often hindered by that potent agent of forgetting—time. This was conclusively demonstrated in the first scientific study of forgetting, the work of a German psychologist named Hermann Ebbinghaus (1850-1909). Ebbinghaus developed a simple test to establish how forgetting operated, which he then tried out on himself. To limit the experiment to the absorption of new knowledge and to minimize the influence of existing information on his results, he devised a system of material to be learned that was completely original—a series of nonsense syllables consisting of a vowel between two consonants, such as ZAT or WAC.

Ebbinghaus made a list of 13 of these nonsense syllables. He then read and reread the list until he could recite it perfectly from memory twice in a

The shape of forgetting
Hermann Ebbinghaus found that most of what is forgotten becomes inaccessible the first few days after it is learned. The amount forgotten then decreases with time. A graph of this process has a characteristic shape known as the Ebbinghaus curve.

HOW QUICKLY DO YOU FORGET?

To see how quickly you forget, study the nonsense words below until you can write out the whole list with no mistakes. Then, each day for the next six days, try to write as many words from the list as you can without referring to this page or to any of your previous attempts.

| DIQ | QOM | WEV | NER | TAH |
| GIW | CUS | BAC | KUD | ROF |

Most people find that by the second day they have forgotten about half the words. After that, the number of new mistakes declines gradually. The Ebbinghaus curve at right shows the average performance of people who took part in a similar six-day experiment. Plot your results on a graph like this and see how they compare.

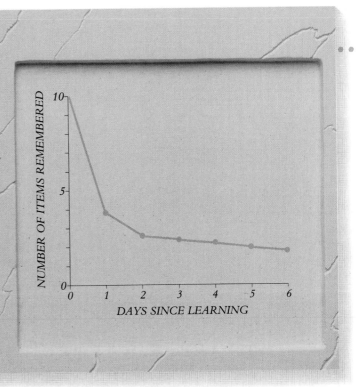

row. Then, at set intervals of time over the next few weeks, he tested himself again to see how many of the syllables he could remember.

From this experiment, which he repeated many times with different sets of nonsense syllables, Ebbinghaus was able to work out how much information is forgotten over time and how quickly it disappears. He discovered that most knowledge is lost rapidly, within the first days after it is learned, but that memory of the remaining knowledge diminishes much more gradually. Those nonsense syllables that he could

remember one month after he first learned them, for example, were still in his memory several months later. The results of Ebbinghaus's experiments have been replicated by other researchers. Plotted on a graph like the one above, they form what is known as the Ebbinghaus forgetting curve.

Little and often

You can never overcome the Ebbinghaus effect totally and retain everything you learn. Yet it does seem possible to permanently imprint upon the memory at least some aspects of any subject. One of the most striking examples of this effect was

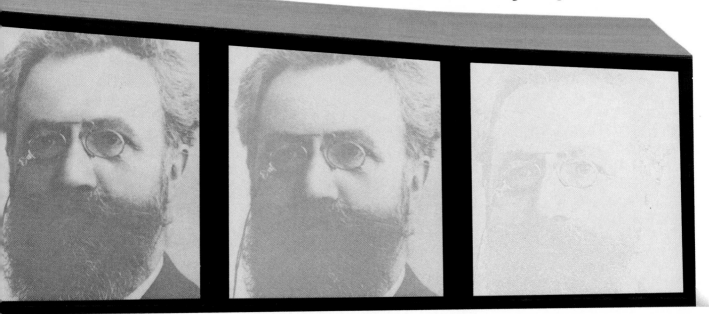

Memory interactions

One memory may obscure or replace another similar memory; two recent birthday celebrations, for example, may become confused in your mind.

INTERFERENCE TEST

To find out for yourself how memories interfere with one another, try this test. First, read the following set of words over to yourself until you know them by heart. Then write the words down from memory.

teddy	witty
jazzy	hobby

Try to hold these words in your mind as you memorize this second, very similar set of words:

tummy	stuffy
baggy	dolly

You will probably find this set harder to recall than the first. Now, do the the same thing with another like-sounding string of words:

nippy	whinny
marry	sissy

This set will take you the longest time of all to learn, since words from the first two will keep popping into your mind. This is the effect of proactive interference, made worse in this test by the similarity of the words. To demonstrate the influence of this similarity, commit a fourth set to memory—this time of numbers:

8055	6099
4011	1077

The set of numbers should be considerably easier to learn because its components are altogether distinct from those of the previous three sets of words.

reported in the findings of Harry Bahrick, who conducted a study of people who had taken Spanish in college. Within three years of graduation, the former students forgot about 60 percent of the Spanish they had learned. Yet, remarkably, during the next 50 years they forgot only an additional 5 percent or so. Similar results have been reported with students of mathematics.

It seems that repeated learning spread out over a long period of time (a process known as distributed practice) offers the best chance of preventing memory decay. Recent research has shown, for example, that

SPECIAL PLACES

Many people place objects they want to be sure to find later in "special places"—locations where the items would never normally be stored. A spare key to the car might be placed in an empty soup tureen, for example, or an extra 20 dollar bill might be stashed under a potted plant. The theory behind this strategy is that the more distinctive the location, the more likely it will be remembered at a later date.

Unfortunately, however, the technique often has just the opposite effect. Because neither keys and soup tureen nor money and potted plants are logically connected, the storage places are easily forgotten. The result: A long and frustrating search.

The only effective way to overcome this problem is to use visualization to create a mental link between the object and the special place where it has been stored. If you want to remember that you put your money under a potted plant, for example, imagine the plant sprouting flowers made of dollar bills. Then, when you later want to find the money you put in that special place, this striking image will immediately come to mind.

students who take successive courses in one particular subject, returning repeatedly to the main concepts, forget less of the material they have learned than those who take a short, but intense, crash course on the same topic.

Interestingly, the studies also show that people who are fast learners do not necessarily have better long-term memories than slow learners. Individuals vary widely in their rates of learning and forgetting; some learn quickly and forget quickly, while others learn quickly but forget slowly.

Meaningful influences

Ebbinghaus's experiments also revealed an intriguing relationship between the nature of learned material and the rate at which it is forgotten. He quickly discovered that memory for more meaningful material, such as speeches and poems, does not decline at the same rate as memory for nonsense syllables. In fact, he had initially chosen to learn more meaningful material for his experiments, but found the material skewed his results because it tended to remain in his memory. Once

he had learned Byron's poem *Don Juan*, for example, he never forgot any of it. The nonsense syllables he invented were much more forgettable.

Mind interference

Apart from the passage of time, probably the most important influence on forgetting is the sometimes disruptive relationship between information newly learned and information already in memory.

This interference takes one of two forms. The first form, called *retroactive* interference, involves forgetting old material when you absorb new material. For example, you might remember the present your brother gave you last Christmas but not the one he gave you three years ago. Memories of the most recent gift have crowded out your remembrance of the earlier one. In the same way, you might remember the name of your new bank manager, whom you met for the first time a week ago, but have difficulty remembering the name of the previous manager, even if you had known him

EARLIEST MEMORIES

How much can you remember from early childhood? Write down as many details as possible about the following:
- The first birthday you can remember
- Your first memorable holiday
- The birth of a younger brother or sister
- Your first day at school
- Favorite preschool toys, clothes, and pets.

After you have done this, check with older family members or friends who were present at the time. You might be surprised to learn that some of your "memories" are largely inaccurate.

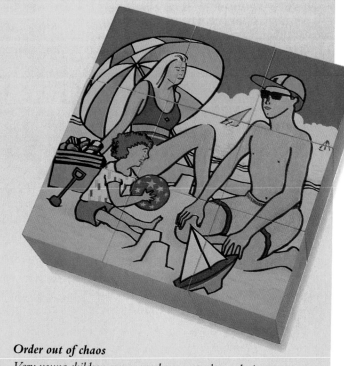

Order out of chaos

Very young children can remember events, but only in a somewhat scrambled order. As they get older, they become more skilled at using their memory and begin to store and recall memories in a more ordered fashion.

for five years. This is not the effect of time—one piece of information has simply been hidden behind another in your memory.

The second form of interference, called *proactive* interference, is the intrusion of existing knowledge on the learning of new information. When you are trying to remember what you need from the supermarket, for instance, it may happen that all you can think of are the items you bought on your previous trip. In the same way, if you are trying to learn French at an evening class, Spanish words that you learned previously in college may keep popping into your mind instead.

This phenomenon has led some psychologists to suggest that Ebbinghaus was at least partially wrong. According to the interference theory of

forgetting, memories never decay or fade away over time; they disappear because they have been actively interfered with by other memories.

Childhood memories

The amount of information people forget varies with their age; memory tends to work most efficiently from adolescence through young adulthood. In general, people's earliest memories for words date from the time they learned to talk in grammatical sentences, which is about the age of three or four. Visual memories, however, can often date from some time before this, as can those involving other senses, such as smell and hearing, and strong emotions, such as fear. People don't normally remember anything from the first two years of life, however, and this absence of memory has been termed childhood (or infantile) amnesia.

Scientists offer several explanations for childhood amnesia. The most likely explanation is that very early observations and feelings are stored in some kind of nonverbal code that is impossible to understand once we learn to talk, and therefore impossible to access as memory. Another factor may be that it is not until children are familiar with the concept of routine in their lives (what usually happens during the morning, for example) that they are able to recognize, and therefore remember, changes from this routine, like the first day at school. It is also true that remembering information is much easier when the information can be fitted into an existing framework. For example, if you read a book about a subject you know well—say computers or movies—you will retain much more of the information than you would if the subject was something totally new to you, such as nuclear physics or Greek. Babies and young

IMPERFECT RECALL

Few experiences are more frustrating than being tantalizingly close to remembering a word—almost seeing its form in your mind—and yet not quite being able to get it out. People tend to describe such a word as being "on the tip of the tongue."

In the course of considerable research into the tip-of-the-tongue (or TOT) phenomenon some interesting facts have come to light:

• A strong link appears to exist between the TOT phenomenon and stress. In a survey of undergraduate psychology majors, 75 percent reported experiencing TOTs more frequently during stressful situations, such as exams.

• On average, adults seem to experience about one TOT a week, but this type of memory failure tends to become more frequent with age.

• During a TOT, people often recall words that are similar in either sound or meaning to the desired word. They are also able to guess the first letter with a high degree of accuracy. An awareness of the last letter is sometimes present.

• A related visual experience is known as a tip-of-the-eye phenomenon. This occurs when you try to recall an image of something from your past, but related images come to mind instead. For example, while trying to visualize your first kitten, you find images of other small furry animals darting into your mind instead.

On the tip of my tongue
When you can't quite remember a word, you may find yourself visualizing its form. You may know whether it is short or long, whether it consists predominantly of curves or straight lines, and perhaps even which letter it begins with. For example, the city that professional baseball's Red Sox call home, is a medium-sized word that has many curves and begins with B.

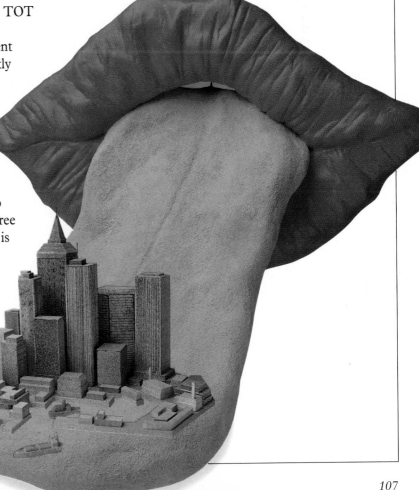

children have not had time to construct a framework of knowledge on any subject, so for them everything is strange and difficult to remember.

Even when early memories do exist, they are often difficult to access immediately, since the stimuli that trigger them can appear illogical to the adult mind. For example, if you try to remind a child of a long-past visit to an elderly aunt by describing the aunt or by providing details of her house or the journey, the child may draw a blank. But when you mention a favorite treat the child was given—perhaps a dish of ice cream—the memories flood back.

Another difficulty is that many apparently clear early memories are not true memories at all, but simply fantasies or recollections of family stories or photographs you have seen.

These factors make summoning up accurate early memories extremely difficult for many adults. Encouragingly, though, research has shown that persistent attempts to recall information can give greatly improved results. This phenomenon is known as hypermnesia. So, if there is an event or particular period in your life that you would like to remember with greater clarity, make frequent attempts to do so and keep a running record of all the information that comes to mind so that you can build on it later.

Memory and aging

Although both science and tradition suggest that memory declines with age, opinions differ widely on the exact nature of this decline and whether there is anything that can be done about it.

One study, for example, has explored the difference between the rates at which memories of

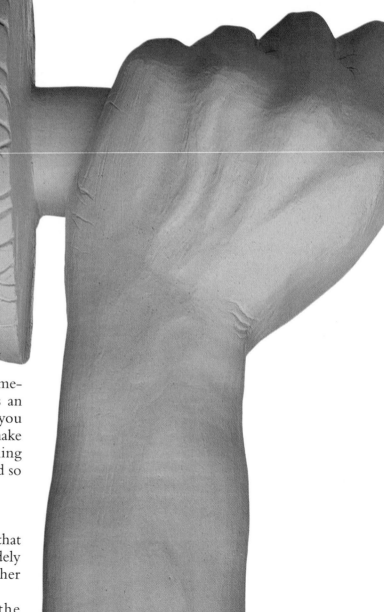

Keep your memory fit
In some ways, human memory is like muscle; exercise can make it healthier and stronger. Word *games, crossword puzzles, and quizzes of all kinds help to keep your memory fit.*

personal experiences (episodic memories) and general knowledge (semantic memories) deteriorate. (For more information on episodic and semantic memory, see pages 31 to 33.) The study showed that although young people perform better in terms of episodic memory, age does not appear to affect semantic memory. Older people sometimes have trouble remembering events in their lives, but they still retain an extensive and useful store of both general and specialized knowledge. Older people are also perfectly capable of absorbing new information and skills, although they may take longer to do so.

In many cases, what appears to be a difficulty in learning or an increased tendency to forget among older people may be something else altogether. For example, older workers may be slower to learn new systems than their younger colleagues, but this slowness is often due as much to a lack of stamina as it is to an age-related difficulty in learning. In addition, illness, bereavement, or isolation can cause anybody to suffer depression, which can in turn affect memory adversely. Older people are just more likely to suffer these problems. If the downward spiral of depression is broken, however, memory can improve dramatically.

In terms of overall intellectual capacity in older people, one factor seems to be universally agreed upon: Those who are socially and mentally active have clearer minds in every way than those who are passive, isolated, and idle. Similarly, enthusiasm, flexibility, curiosity, and a genuine interest in other people all have a strong and positive influence on brain function, and therefore on memory. As with so many of the different skills we acquire throughout life, the most important rule for the preservation of memory seems to be "use it or lose it."

STAY BRIGHT

Without maintenance your memory may deteriorate with age. Here are five key tips for keeping your memory in peak condition:

1. Stay physically healthy. Eat a nutritious diet and get plenty of exercise. If you are inactive, you may be able to remember as much as your active friends but you will not be able to recall it as quickly. By becoming more active, you will increase your speed of recall. Even gentle exercise such as walking can be beneficial.

2. Expect the best of your memory. Never assume that mental deterioration is an inevitable consequence of old age. If your memory begins to deteriorate for no apparent reason, make an appointment with your doctor. Many physiological disorders—like anemia, for example—can cause memory confusion.

3. Don't be passive. Avoid spending too much time in mind-dulling ways, such as watching television; lack of mental activity encourages the loss of mental capacity. Look for stimulation all the time—for example, in reading, doing crossword puzzles, or craft hobbies. These activities will help keep your memory in much better working order.

4. Meet interesting people. Talking to other people and exchanging information, ideas, and reminiscences is important for keeping yourself mentally fit. If you live alone, make a particular effort to keep in touch with friends and neighbors. Find a group activity or a club that reflects your interests. If you are retired, seek out some suitable volunteer work, perhaps in a hospital or a school for handicapped children.

5. Make full use of memory aids. These can either be simple ones, such as making lists and writing notes to yourself, or commercial devices, such as diaries, telephones with computer memories for often-used numbers, electronic personal organizers, and pill dispensers with integral timers.

MEMORY LOSS

Most people forget things occasionally. When memory loss begins to occur on a more frequent basis, however, there may well be a medical cause. People who lose their ability to remember large amounts of information are said to be suffering from amnesia.

The word "amnesia" often conjures up the image of the much-used film scenario: A character wakes up after a blow on the head and cannot remember who he or she is. This form of memory loss does exist, but it is comparatively rare. Much more common is amnesia that occurs gradually, as a result of disease, advancing age, or long-term alcohol abuse. People thus affected rarely lose their sense of identity or completely forget their past. Instead, they have great difficulty acquiring new information.

Having amnesia is said to be like living in a dream with no feeling of continuity and no ability to plan for the future. Imagine what it must be like to be unable to remember what you did a few hours ago or to read through to the end of a book and not remember its beginning.

Memory disorders

One of the most common causes of memory loss in older people is Alzheimer's disease. In this progressive disorder, brain cells are lost more rapidly than usual through decay. An increased tendency to forget appointments or messages and to lose things is often the first symptom of the illness. As the disease progresses, factual information is lost from the long-term memory as well. Affected people may have growing difficulty in finding appropriate words and defining even simple objects. For example, when asked to describe an ox, they may become confused and begin to give a description of an elephant. At its most severe, Alzheimer's disease

Stop the clock
Brain damage caused by long-term alcohol abuse can make it impossible for a person to absorb any new information. When this happens, time effectively comes to a standstill. An affected person may, for example, become mentally stranded in time and lose touch with current events.

causes dementia and leaves its victims unable to care for themselves in their daily lives.

Another form of memory loss, called Korsakoff's syndrome, occurs as a result of chronic alcoholism. Drinking too much alcohol and having too little to eat over a considerable period results in a vitamin deficiency that damages important structures within the brain. Over time the person becomes less able to learn new information and grows increasingly forgetful. Severely affected people can only recall memories that they learned before their brains were damaged; they do not accumulate memories of personal experiences as they normally would. During a typical day, people suffering from Korsakoff's syndrome live in an environment

SLEEPING MEMORY

People with amnesia are able to learn, but they have no memory of acquiring the new information. A good analogy for the way amnesics learn may be the kind of learning that takes place while an ordinary person is unconscious. Surgery patients, for example, are unable to consciously recall any of the events that took place while they were anesthetized. However, a postoperative change in attitude toward a doctor has sometimes been traced to something the physician said during surgery.

Swiss psychiatrist Edouard Claparède (1873-1940) was the first to demonstrate this feature of amnesia. He unkindly secreted a pin in his hand before shaking hands with one of his amnesic patients. The following day the patient had no conscious memory of what had happened, but was unusually reluctant to shake hands. The unfortunate patient could not express why he didn't want to shake hands, but speculated that "sometimes pins are hidden in people's palms."

full of strangers. They are unable to recognize people they see every day, or even those they have met a few minutes earlier. Nor can they remember what day it is, even if constantly reminded. But people with Korsakoff's syndrome usually do retain many of the skills they acquired before their brain damage occurred. They may, for example, remember how to read and write, or drive a car.

Dealing with memory loss

You can help yourself overcome a slight memory loss with mental exercises. Keeping the mind active and challenged has been shown to improve memory skills (see the "Stay bright" box on page 109). If you think that your memory is failing through illness, however, you should contact your doctor without delay. Medical intervention can sometimes reduce the rate of memory loss associated with progressive diseases such as Alzheimer's.

Missing memories
Memories lost after a blow on the head usually return in time. But some accident victims have a permanent blank about the incident itself, because they blacked out before the experience was transferred to long-term memory.

DO YOU REALLY REMEMBER?

SOME EVENTS leave particularly vivid memories. But a vivid memory does not necessarily provide an accurate account of what really happened. Studies have shown that most people remember even exceptional incidents inaccurately.

One explanation for this is that it is nearly impossible to recall events objectively. Your memories are shaped by your subjective view and also by the time that has passed between the event and your recollection of it. Time and personal viewpoint inevitably change the way you remember what happened. By being aware of the influences that can distort your memories, however, you can learn to allow for them and improve your recall.

Conflicting memories

The most dangerous aspect of vivid but false memories is that they are so convincing. You are certain you can remember exactly what took place—you can even "see" it clearly in your mind's eye. Yet comparing notes with another person who was present at the time may reveal huge discrepancies. You might believe that your memory of a particularly enjoyable day some years ago is accurate: "I remember the day well. It was lovely and sunny. Remember how John and Audrey complained about how far we cycled?" But your companion remembers the event totally differently: "Actually, it was a cloudy day. John wasn't with us. Audrey was with Scott that day." Many an argument between friends has stemmed from such situations, with each person utterly convinced that his or her own recalled version is the accurate one.

You may be unaware that your memory has made mistakes because you use one incorrect memory to confirm the supposed accuracy of

A street crime

Most people with normal memories do not remember everything they see. Instead, they tend to remember a small portion of an event. Imagine you are on vacation in an unfamiliar city. As you walk around the town you come across the scene shown here. Would you notice the pickpocket at work? If so, you would be unlikely to remember what the other people were doing at the same time. Look at this scene for 30 seconds and then turn to page 118.

DISTORTED MEMORIES

Here is an exercise in memory distortion. Examine the drawings below for about 30 seconds. Then close the book and try to reproduce each drawing as accurately as you can. Do your drawings before you read on.

BANJO

TREE

DRUM

HOOK

FIGURE FOUR

When you compare your drawings with the originals, you will probably find they are less abstract and more suggestive of the words under each of the original images—for instance, your "tree" probably looks much more like a tree than the original image did. Your brain made a link between the drawings and the labels attached. Your memory of the original drawing was then distorted to fit in with the verbal information. Now, turn to page 140 to see how others have drawn these same images when given a different set of captions.

another. For example, you might say, "I'm sure I met you on Tuesday because I took my car to be serviced that day." In reality, you may have taken the car to be serviced on a Wednesday, and both memories are incorrect.

In everyday life, such small memory failures usually lead to only minor inconveniences. When you are an eyewitness to a crime or accident, however, the amount of detail you can recall accurately becomes an important issue. People attending a court case are often amazed at the discrepancies in the testimony of different eyewitnesses to the same crime. It seems to imply that someone is lying. But research into eyewitness testimony by psychologist Elizabeth Loftus suggests that the truth is not always distorted intentionally. Discrepancies may arise because a witness is recalling a sincere, but inaccurate, memory.

When an eyewitness points to the accused during a trial and says, "He did it," the jury will almost certainly find that person guilty. Thousands of people every year are suspects in cases in which the only critical evidence against them is eyewitness identification. Eyewitness testimony is the most damning piece of evidence that a defendant can be faced with, and yet it is often unreliable.

Seeing the whole picture

As an eyewitness, you may remember an accident or a crime incorrectly simply because you did not see the whole scene. Maybe you witnessed a car accident but did not see the dog crossing the road

FOUR FACES

Try this memory test: Look at the four faces below for no longer than 10 seconds (just as if they had passed you in the street). Now, turn to page 116. Which of these faces is shown there?

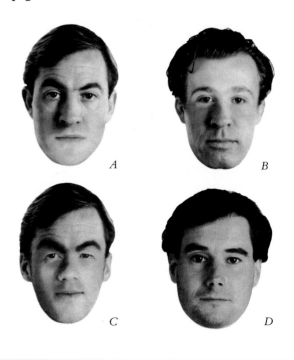

A

B

C

D

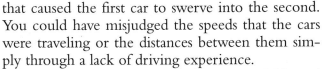

Speed of thought
Accidents happen without warning. Eyewitnesses are usually caught by surprise at the rapidly occurring events and have little time to take in everything. They remember only parts of what they saw, then later use these few details to reconstruct what happened. How much detail would you remember from the accident shown here?

that caused the first car to swerve into the second. You could have misjudged the speeds that the cars were traveling or the distances between them simply through a lack of driving experience.

A crime or accident usually happens quickly and without warning. During this brief time, your short-term memory is bombarded by information it receives from your senses: sights, sounds, smells, and textures. Because there is too much information to be processed at once, your brain picks out the major points and stores only a brief synopsis of the event—fragments of the whole picture, such as "dog," "automobile," "moving," and "crash"—in your long-term memory. Thus, only part of what you see, hear, smell, and feel can be remembered. To recall the whole event, your mind reconstructs the scene using these small pieces of information.

The mind also uses scripted information (see pages 36 to 39) to reconstruct memories. These scripts provide a framework on which to build a memory fitting what you expect to happen in any situation. When parts of the story are missing, your mind subconsciously fills in the gaps and you remember this completed version as though it actually occurred. Each person, of course, tends to

reconstruct his or her memory of an event in a different way. All memories have a personal bias.

Observant people make better eyewitnesses because they pay more attention to what is happening around them at any time. If you are an observant person, you will store more fragments of information and thus will need to make fewer guesses when you reconstruct a memory.

Effects of time
The passage of time may also change a memory. Even if you have carefully observed a scene initially, your memory of the event can be subsequently distorted by later pieces of information. You may experience retroactive interference, where a new piece of information replaces an old memory. For example, you may witness a red car leaving the scene of a bank robbery at high speed. On the way home, you see another speeding red car—a completely different make—which you then substitute in your memory for the earlier one. Or, you may experience proactive interference and combine your memory of the bank robbery with something you heard in a news report about another robbery several days earlier.

Over time, a memory that is not immediately recalled can become more difficult to remember accurately because of interference from other memories. As detail becomes more difficult to recall, your mind begins to make guesses to fill the gaps left by missing information and your memory of an event becomes increasingly distorted.

Memories, however, do not always fade with time. Sometimes a memory becomes clearer with time as more and more details and their interactions are recalled. By recalling or thinking about a situation over and over again it may become reinforced or sharpened in your mind.

But continually recalling an event in an attempt to remember more about it can also introduce inaccuracies. It may change and become a biased version of what really happened. For example, in conversation with another witness you might be told that the driver of a blue car was seen running from the scene of the crime. This statement assigns a degree of guilt to the driver in your mind. You might then "remember" more negative statements about the driver's behavior than before. Alternatively, if you heard that the driver had rushed away to get help, you might remember more positive aspects of his behavior than before.

Leading questions

When recalling information about a crime or accident, leading questions may entice you to produce different versions of the truth and even alter your memory of the event. Imagine that you are being asked questions about a car crash you had seen. Would you answer the question "Did you see a child distract the driver?" any differently than the question "Did you see the child distract the driver?" The second question assumes that there was a child distracting the driver. This might influence the way you recall the accident. If an investigator referred to the "speeding car" in a question about a car accident, your perception of the event may become colored. In reality, the car may have been traveling well within the speed limit before the accident. Similarly, using words like "smashed" instead of "bumped" may exaggerate the severity of the accident in your memory.

A question phrased in a certain way could shake your confidence as an eyewitness. For example, imagine that you saw an accident from a distance of 50 feet. If someone questioning you about the accident refers to this distance as moderately far, rather than moderately near, you might begin to believe that you saw the incident relatively poorly, instead of relatively clearly. Your memory of the event may gradually change as a result. The more knowledgeable an investigator appears to be about the accident or crime being discussed, the greater will be the effect of any leading questions on the memories of an eyewitness.

Elizabeth Loftus investigated the extent to which leading questions can influence eyewitness accounts. She showed her subjects a videotape

DO YOU RECOGNIZE THIS FACE?

You have looked at the four faces on page 114 for 10 seconds. Can you say for sure whether the face below is face A, B, C, or D?

You probably identified this illustration as face A. In reality, however, you have not seen this face before. It seems familiar only because it is composed of features from two of the previous faces; the nose, eyes, forehead, and hair came from face A, but the mouth and chin belong to face B. The original question also implied that you had seen this face before. Your memory is easily confused by a leading question and an image that seems familiar.

VIOLENT EFFECTS

Does violence make a crime more or less memorable to an eyewitness? A victim of a violent crime is under extreme stress. Research has shown that although mild stress can heighten a person's memory of an event, extreme stress can have the opposite effect.

In the late 1970s, psychologists Brian Clifford and Jane Scott tested the effects of violence on memory. They played two videos of the same story to two different groups; one video was violent, the other was not. The violent scene consisted of a policeman restraining a struggling man. The nonviolent scene showed the same two people arguing verbally. The beginning and the end were the same in both videos. After viewing the film, the members of each group were asked to describe what they had seen. They remembered consistently less of the violent version than they did of the nonviolent version. It seems, then, that violence can have a detrimental effect on memory.

Weapon focus
You might think that if someone brandished a weapon at you, the details of that event, and the face of your assailant, would be unforgettable. Research shows, however, that in a violent crime, the weapon often becomes the focus of attention. People concentrate on the weapon to such an extent that they take in less information about other details of the crime.

recording of a car accident and afterwards asked them to estimate how fast a car in the video had been going when it "passed the barn." Later, they were asked to describe the accident scene shown on the video. A sizable number of them mentioned seeing a barn, but there had been no barn in the video. The subjects had remembered the information supplied in the question more vividly than the actual event itself.

When your memory of an event is incomplete, constant questioning by lawyers or the police may compel you to provide concrete answers by making guesses for what you can't quite recall. You may then begin to incorporate these guesses into your original memory of the event.

Shaken confidence

Confidence in your own memory of a face can be undermined or enhanced by leading questions during an investigation. Imagine you are an eyewitness to a crime. You are led to believe that a suspect is among the members of a police lineup. Your task is simply to provide a positive identification. If anyone in the lineup is similar in appearance to the suspect, you will, of course, identify him or her with great certainty. If, instead, you are told only that the suspect *may be* in the lineup, you probably will not be as confident about making an identification. Thus, you will be less likely to make a false identification. People are more likely to feel they have seen a face before if they are expecting to see it.

Limiting distortions

It is unlikely that you will ever escape all the influences—time, other memories, conflicting information—that can skew your memory of a particular event. Yet, by being aware of these influences, you can minimize their distorting effects. To ensure that a memory is accurate, you need, initially, to be observant. When you are confident about what you saw or heard at the time, you will be less likely to let the opinion of others alter your remembrance of the event.

ARE YOU A RELIABLE EYEWITNESS?

Deep down, everybody would like to believe that he or she would make an excellent eyewitness. The reality is often very different. Most people would have great difficulty producing a truly detailed and accurate eyewitness account of a dramatic scene or event. The most reliable accounts are produced by people who are generally observant.

How good a witness would you be? In this section, you looked at a number of pictures. Without looking back, test your powers of observation by answering questions relating to these pictures in the boxes below and at right. Write down your answers. Then, turn to page 141 to see how good an eyewitness you really are.

While you are unlikely to be able to remember everything that happens during a particular event, you can improve your memory of the episode by focusing on a few details. If you witness a crime, for example, try to memorize specific features of the perpetrator's face. If a vehicle is involved in a crime or accident, make sure you know its color, make, and, if possible, its license plate number. To aid your memory, write down as many details of the incident as you can, as soon as possible.

A STREET CRIME

You spent 30 seconds looking at the large picture of a city street scene at the beginning of this section (pages 112 and 113). In this scene, you noticed a pickpocket in action. But how much do you remember about the other people in the picture? Without looking back, try to answer the following questions. You will find the solutions to these questions on page 141.

1. What was the woman in the beige jacket carrying?

2. What was the pickpocket's victim wearing?

3. Who, apart from yourself, seemed to notice the pickpocket?

4. What color was the bicycle?

5. What was the woman wearing the orange sweater carrying?

6. Why didn't the victim notice the pickpocket?

7. How many people were having their photograph taken?

8. What was the man in the black leather jacket doing?

9. How many people were carrying umbrellas?

10. How many people were wearing yellow: one, two, or three?

Identity parade
You witnessed a pickpocket at work at the beginning of this section. The police have arrested a suspect and have asked you to identify him from this lineup. Who would you choose? Turn to page 141 to find out which man it was.

A

TRAFFIC ACCIDENT

Without looking back, try to answer these questions about the accident sequence shown earlier in this section. The answers are on page 141.

1. What was the color of the second car that passed by?

2. Did the traffic lights change?

3. What colors were the two cars involved in the accident?

4. Was one car turning to the right?

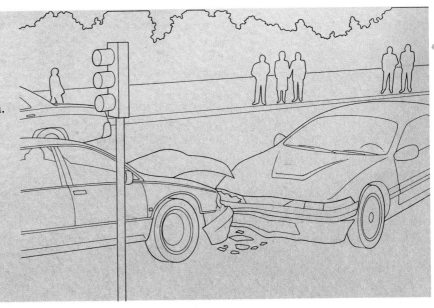

B   C   D   E

CHAPTER FOUR

BUILD UP YOUR SKILLS

NO MATTER HOW impressive your knowledge of memory-improving techniques, there is no substitute for the practical experience of actually applying them day to day in learning new pieces of information. In other words, the theory is not much use without a fair amount of practice. You can build up your memory skills in countless different ways, whether you are digesting the contents of a company's complicated annual report or simply remembering the name of someone to whom you have just been introduced.

You will probably find it most productive if you can practice memory techniques frequently, but for brief periods of time. It is also helpful to come at specific memory problems from as many different angles as you can. If you have memorized a list and can recite it start to finish confidently and without errors, try reciting the list in reverse order. Practicing the material in this way will not only reinforce your understanding of it, it will also allow you flexibility in recalling the information, so you will not be limited to dredging up the entire list to remember just one item which happens to be near the end.

Most people lead increasingly busy lives in which there never seems to be enough time to accomplish everything that needs doing. But there are almost always small pockets of dead time, even in the busiest of days—times when it is not practical to be accomplishing much other than to muse aimlessly. Practicing and polishing your memory techniques is an ideal activity during such moments. Fortunately, your memory is portable and instantly accessible at all times of day.

While there are no physical short-cuts to great memory power—no miracle drugs that will produce infallible recall—there are a number of sensible habits you can adopt to provide the best foundation on which to build. Keeping yourself fit is a commonsense measure, as is the avoidance of brain-damaging substances—including excessive quantities of alcohol. It is also worth noting that you don't have to abandon altogether the use of external memory aids such as phone lists, notepads, or adhesive notes. Above all, don't lose your sense of humour. Keeping your memories striking and funny will make them much easier to

APPLY THE PRINCIPLES OF ORDER AND CONNECTEDNESS
TO YOUR MEMORIES AND YOUR RECALL WILL
STEADILY IMPROVE.

USE WHAT YOU HAVE LEARNED

MEMORY TECHNIQUES CAN help you learn and remember almost any material. This is true even when what you wish to learn does not conveniently lend itself to one particular technique. In cases like this, you can combine several different methods, adapting them to suit the material. As you get used to choosing the right technique—or coming up with the right combination of techniques—the process becomes much easier.

A working advantage
When you are giving a speech or delivering a report, you will make a much greater impact if you produce relevant information from memory—sales figures, for example—without stopping to refer to notes or files. By identifying in advance some crucial points you want to produce effortlessly, and using a combination of memory techniques to remember them, you can give yourself a terrific advantage in any business meeting.

Suppose you think it would be impressive to be able to recall precise figures for the number of items your company sold in particular years: 1.1 million items in 1988, 0.8 million in 1989, 1.6 million in 1990, and 1.4 million in 1991. It would be so easy—and embarrassing—to confuse the figures and link them with the wrong years. You must not only remember the sales figures, using the techniques you have already learned (see "A head for figures" on pages 92 to 99), but you have to link them unmistakably to the appropriate years.

You might easily remember the figure for 1988 because of the doubles; two 1s and two 8s. So concentrate your attention on the other figures that are less memorable. Using visual imagery for numbers (as described on page 95), you might imagine the 0.8 as an orange wearing eyeglasses. By also putting a pair of glasses on a balloon on a stick, you could remember the year—'89. And by visualizing a bespectacled orange waving a bespectacled balloon, you can link the two numbers inextricably in your mind.

By thinking of the 90 percent your 16-year-old daughter just scored on her mathematics test, you can recall the 1.6 million items your company sold in 1990. You might remember that the sales figure for the final year, 1991, is 1.4 because the number of your apartment is 14. Visualize a rocket crashing through your apartment door—that will link the 1 for 1991 to the 14. (You are unlikely to confuse it with 1981 or 1971, so the 1 is enough to remember the whole year.)

Remember that address
For addresses and phone numbers, most people rely on keeping an address book. But you will not always have your address book when you need it. Think of the advantages of not having to look up addresses and phone numbers all the time. If you can memorize them, you can turn your address book into an emergency backup to your memory. Reeling off the addresses and numbers

unaided will also, of course, impress others and save time. And it will ensure that it is much less of a disaster if you ever lose your address book.

Say you wanted to link your business client John Ruzak to his home address: 428 Gospel Street, Arlington Heights, Illinois 60005. To visualize his name, you could think of him hiking with a large

rucksack; to link this to Gospel Street, have him singing as he walks along. The lyric of the song is "four times two equals eight," which you sing to yourself in gospel tones. Then visualize him, with his rucksack, singing the number song and climbing a giant letter A. The climbing will cue Heights and the A will act as a cue for Arlington. You will remember that he lives in Illinois, so link the code 60005 to the state, using similar techniques.

Of course, you can often remember many elements of a person's address or phone number without effort, simply because the information has become familiar to you through repetitive use over a long period of time.

Get into the habit of noticing which parts you always forget,

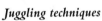

Juggling techniques

To develop your memory skills you need to use all the methods described in this volume, often combining a few techniques to perform one memory task.

Through practice you will increase your ability to juggle several techniques at once and increase the speed at which you learn and recall facts.

CUES FOR SPEAKING

Just like many people, you may be filled with dread at the thought of giving a speech to even a small audience. You imagine yourself making mistakes, stumbling over your words, and forgetting what you wanted to say. But you can minimize the chances of such mishaps. First, prepare an outline of your speech so that your thoughts are organized. Make a note of any numbers or quotes you would like to use, as these are probably the things you will find most difficult to remember. Rehearse the speech standing in front of an imaginary audience, until you feel confident with your delivery.

To give yourself confidence while speaking in public, write down the main points you wish to make on cue cards. You can then refer to the cards as you talk. Cue cards are used by many experienced speech makers. The cards are to the speech maker what the prompter is to an actor; they jog your memory at the right moment.

People do not want to listen to you reading aloud, they want to hear you speak, so keep the amount you write to a minimum. Limit yourself to 10 cards. Write headings in large letters so that you can see them easily. Each card should carry a number of headings for the key points in the order you want to make them.

On your first cue card you might have three prompting words: One for the title of your speech, one for the punch line of the joke you will use to catch the attention of your audience, and one for the first key point you wish to make. Once you have completed the sections referred to on one card, refer to the next.

and apply a memory technique to them as the need arises, until there is no longer a problem.

The practical applications of good memory skills extend to first aid. Imagine that you are attending a course as part of your training to be a flight attendant. You find some of the material difficult to remember: Whether to use an acid or an alkali on a bee sting, how to treat a sprain, and whether you should raise or lower someone's head in case of fainting. To remember the various treatments you could either develop your own rhymes or mnemonics, or learn existing ones. For example, by learning the phrase "If pale raise the tail; if red raise the head," you will know exactly what action to take when someone faints. Similarly, by learning the acronym "RICE," standing for Rest, Ice, Compression, and Elevation, you will know how to treat a sprained ankle.

You could develop your own mnemonic for the treatment of bee and wasp stings. By knowing that vinegar is acidic and bicarbonate alkaline, you could combine the first letters of "bee" and "bicarbonate" to remind you to treat bee stings with bicarbonate, or anything alkaline. And you can simply match the first letters of the words "vinegar" and "wasp" to give you "VW"—the famous trademark of Volkswagen cars.

Preparing for a vacation

It is easy to forget things when packing for a family vacation, but if you use a few memory techniques, the job becomes much simpler. They can help you to overcome that nagging doubt in your mind. First, organize your thoughts by writing down the main categories of items you will need: underwear and clothing for all occasions, toiletries, medication, photography equipment, entertainment for the kids, and papers such as tickets, traveler's checks, and insurance documents. Create a mnemonic to help you remember all the categories so that you can check them off in your mind as you pack. In this case you could reorganize the first letters of the words Underwear, Toiletries, Medication, Photography, Entertainment, and Papers to make the acronym "MUPPET."

Using another mnemonic, you can remember the items in each category. For example, under the heading "papers" you might want to remember tickets, money, traveler's checks, passport, and vaccination certificates. You could use the first letter of each item to make an acrostic: "Toasted Marshmallows Taste Perfectly Vile." This will provide you with your mental checklist. By spending some time developing a thorough system, you can then use it every time you pack for a trip.

A lesson in history

As part of an American history course, you may need to learn the names of the first 10 U.S. presidents in the order in which they held office. They were George Washington, John Adams, Thomas Jefferson, James Madison, James Monroe, John Quincy Adams, Andrew Jackson, Martin Van

TIPS FROM WAITERS

Bar and restaurant staff need to remember hundreds of drink and food orders in the course of a week. When bartenders take a drink order, they immediately reach for the appropriate glasses and put them on the bar. The sizes and shapes of these serve as visual reminders for the order. When mixing a cocktail, bartenders use their memory of the correct color of the drink to prepare it with the right combination of ingredients. When experienced bartenders are given glasses through which the color of the drink cannot be seen, they make more mistakes in the mixing process than usual.

John Conran, a waiter from Boulder, Colorado, became famous for his outstanding memory. He could remember 20 complete dinner orders without making a single note. On hearing an order, he immediately organized it, grouping repeats together. He developed a code of letters representing each item on the menu—B for blue cheese dressing, T for thousand island—and formed them into nonsense words to remember part of the order. Using visual imagery, he also linked clients with entrées. He might, for example, visualize beefy jowls on someone who ordered a steak, and a spaghetti hairdo on someone who ordered pasta. This imagery acted as a trigger allowing him to recall the rest of the order.

You are what you eat
Waiters often use visual imagery to link a dish with the client who ordered it. Someone who had asked for duck might be imagined with a beak; someone who ordered pork, a snout. Seeing the client's face then acts as a cue to this visual image and enables the waiter to recall the order.

Buren, William Henry Harrison, and John Tyler (pictured left to right, below). By using a combination of memory techniques—and an element of fun—you can commit this list of names to memory quite easily. Here are some examples of how you might approach the task.

First, you can use visual imagery to help you memorize each name. For example, to remind yourself of the first president, imagine the capital of the U.S., Washington, D.C. Think of a man dressed only in a fig leaf to remind you of the name Adams. You could use the same image for the second Adams in the list, but this time have him holding a quince (a hard-fleshed yellow fruit) to remember Quincy Adams. The words "deaf person" sound like the name Jefferson. You could imagine Thomas Jefferson holding a hearing trumpet to his ear. Remind yourself of the name Madison by thinking of a man who is mad at his son: "Mad at son" sounds like Madison. The name

of the fifth president on the list would be more memorable if you imagined a man walking arm in arm with Marilyn Monroe. Try this method for yourself with the remaining names in the list: Jackson, van Buren, Harrison, and Tyler.

Putting it in order

Once you have worked out a visual image for each name, you need to develop a system that enables you to keep them in the correct order. You could do this in a number of ways. One way is to employ the method of the loci (see pages 74 to 79). Using a familiar location, such as your home, place the 10 images so that you come across them in chronological order as you walk around the house. For example, when you open the front door you will see the first image you created, a model of Washington, D.C., by the phone in the hall. Then you will see Adams, dressed only in his fig leaf, loitering in the doorway to the kitchen, and Jefferson, the "deaf

person," sitting on top of the stove straining to hear what you are saying. Madison would be arguing with his son, who is standing in the sink, and so on. The last image you will come across in your imaginary walk around your home will be the one you created for the 10th president, John Tyler. Perhaps his name would be represented by a man laying carpet tiles on the dining room ceiling.

Another equally effective way of remembering the order correctly would be to use the peg system described on pages 72 and 73. To apply this technique, combine each president's image with words that rhyme with the numbers one to 10; one is bun, two is shoe, three is tree for example. Imagine Washington, D.C. on top of a large bun, Adams wearing only a fig leaf and one shoe, Jefferson as the deaf person sitting in a tree. For the fourth name, Madison, you could imagine the angry man slamming a door while arguing with his son. Try this technique for yourself with the rest of your images. When it comes to recalling each president you can remember his name and position by thinking of what the door (number four), for example, was doing in your mental image.

The memory techniques described in this volume can be adapted for use on any material, no matter how lengthy or intricate. There are almost limitless ways you can combine techniques to overcome any memory problem, whether you want to remember the amount in your bank account, or the names of all the people in a large company. All it takes is a little time, effort, and imagination.

Rock solid memories

To remember the names of the first 10 presidents in the order they held office, you need to combine several memory techniques. By taking time to carve out images, you will fix them in your memory and be less likely to forget them.

STUDYING TECHNIQUES

It is not only full-time students who need to study for examinations. Many people must pass accounting exams or study for real estate licensing exams, for example, to progress in their chosen career.

The way you study has a profound effect on how much you learn and remember. Surveys have shown that it is not always the brightest students who do the best academically. College students with high, middle, and low grade averages differ not in ability but in learning strategies. To achieve your full potential you need to adopt an effective study system. Many systems have been devised, but they all share

one strategy—to first identify and then tackle your weaknesses in your chosen subject. One such technique, the Murder system, is described below.

Study time

People vary in the amount of time that they can spend studying effectively. Some can concentrate for half an hour, others for several hours at a stretch. To compare the effectiveness of varying lengths of study time, researchers asked one group of students to study for one hour a day, and another group for four hours a day in two-hour sessions. Although the

Studying is MURDER

However you feel about having to study, you will want to make the most of your study time. Try the Murder study system described here. Murder is an acronym of six stages: Mood, Understand, Recall, Digest, Expand, and Review.

Understand
To learn any information, you must first understand it.

Understand

To learn the principles behind any material you are studying, first identify those areas you find most difficult to understand. Read through the material, highlighting tricky parts of the text, then devote more of your time to working with these.

Mood
You need to be in the right mood to concentrate.

Mood

Studying at a particular time every day will turn the work into a habit, then you will be more likely to be in the right mood to concentrate. Take short breaks when your concentration wavers.

Recall
Recalling facts reinforces what you have learned.

Recall

After reading a section, test yourself to see how much you remember. Write down a list of the important points made in the text. Ask yourself how each point relates to the next.

second group spent four times as many hours working, they learned only twice as much the other group. It seems then that the saying "little and often is best" holds true—your memory can retain more information when you limit yourself to shorter periods of study.

To hold on to more of what you have learned you need to recall, or review, the material you are studying at regular intervals. While working, you should stop every 10 minutes to review what you have just learned. To do this you could, for example, make a note of the key points. Ideally, you should review the

material again one day, one week, one month, and four months after you have first learned it.

During study you are often required to read books that contain a great deal of information. One effective way of remembering the contents of any book is to make a list of the main points as you read. The headings provide cues that allow you to recall information that falls under each one. If you memorize the headings you will be able to recall much of the book's content. To help you remember the order of the headings you might, for example, make an acronym using the first letter from each of them.

Expand
Try to apply and evaluate the information you have learned.

Expand
To develop your knowledge and increase your recall, ask yourself questions about the material you have learned. How can you apply it? How would you go about explaining the material? Give examples of the principles explained in the text.

Digest
Read more about those areas where your knowledge is patchy.

Digest
Try to find more information on those parts of the material that you do not understand or find difficult to remember. Discuss and analyze your difficulty with someone.

Review
Identify errors and make appropriate changes in your study habits.

Review
Continually monitor your progress by checking summaries or lists of important points that you have written from memory against the original material.

BETTER EVERY DAY

IMAGINE READING A MANUAL on learning to swim that is full of information, illustrations, diagrams, and helpful hints. It contains simple instructions on how to get into the water, as well as detailed descriptions of the most advanced techniques and strokes. No matter how many times you read the book, however, you will never learn to swim until you have practiced in the water—just as you will never become thin by reading a diet book or wealthy by studying a get-rich-quick guide.

In the same way, this volume offers a wealth of advice on how to improve your memory. It includes myriad useful tricks and techniques, such as visualizing and chunking, that have been proven to be effective. But these will only work if you make the effort to put them into practice.

Adapting the systems

Many times you will find memory-improving techniques most useful if you can adapt them to your own particular circumstances. For example, the chapter on number power contains lots of tips for remembering telephone numbers. Perhaps there aren't many telephone numbers you need to remember, but your job involves dealing with serial or registration numbers of some kind. In this case, the same techniques could be applied. Similarly, you may have little difficulty with people's names, but find it impossible to keep straight all the model names of the products manufactured by your company. Again, adapt the appropriate technique to your own needs. It is a good idea to make a note of the memory problems that repeatedly present you with difficulties: Next time you catch yourself declaring "Oh, I can never remember that," jot it down. Later, when you have some free time, you can attack your list of perennial problems.

This book provides you with raw materials. Now it is up to you to set up a system that suits you. You are the only one who is aware of where your memory skills are weakest and only you will be able to appreciate your rate of improvement. Follow the "Seven-day memory plan" on page 131 to get you started.

To give yourself the greatest possible advantage, exercise your memory regularly by bringing particular collections of facts and figures to mind at will. Those moments when you are daydreaming or just staring into space are ideal for this kind of exercise; try it the next time you are waiting for a bus or train, standing in line for an automatic teller machine, or waiting in the supermarket checkout line. Keep practicing and testing yourself to keep your memory muscles strong.

Climbing new heights
Like scaling a mountain, learning new memory skills can be daunting at the start. But once you begin the climb, you will be surprised at just how much you can achieve. You can conquer a poor memory for faces, overcome a block about names, or remember facts you never thought you could.

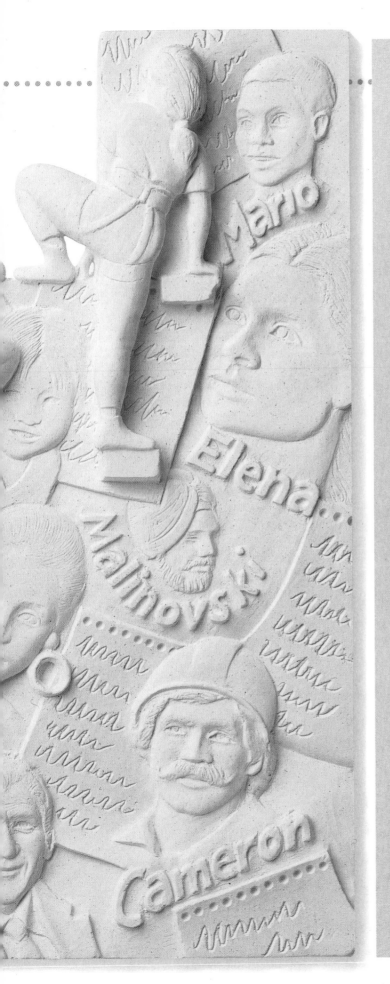

THE SEVEN-DAY MEMORY PLAN

This is a crash course to get you started on genuine memory improvement. Spending just 30 to 45 minutes each day on these tasks will produce significant, measurable improvement.

Day 1 Rehearse your peg words—one/bun, two/shoe, three/tree, and so on—and practice them in remembering a random list of 10 words. Give each number from one to 10 an equivalent image—one/a rocket, two/a swan, and so on. Then practice these, visualizing short mind movies for three four-digit numbers.

Day 2 Choose two places that you could use to locate memory items in using the method of the loci. Rehearse the places by walking around them in your mind until you are confident you can visualize them in order. Then choose two lists of objects and memorize them by placing them around your chosen locations.

Day 3 Practice remembering a list of 10 names —find them by opening the phone book at random. Form a visual image for each name. Then choose five phone numbers, and memorize them by chunking and then forming personal associations with each chunk.

Day 4 Revise and combine the techniques, so that you can memorize a list of names and numbers in order. Work out which techniques will apply to this problem, then use them to link and order the names and numbers.

Day 5 Write a list of the memory objectives that you would like to achieve. Would you like to recall the contents of your address book, or the complete list of Oscar winners? What numbers would you like to have at your fingertips? Applying the techniques you have practiced, begin to work systematically through your list.

Day 6 Continue working through your memory list. How much of the material that you committed to memory on day 5 can you recall?

Day 7 Push yourself. Give yourself 10 minutes to memorize a list of 25 words, and another 10 minutes to memorize a 20-digit number. Once you have accomplished these tasks, you will have memory confidence for life.

GETTING IN SHAPE

It is true that a healthy body equals a healthy mind. Mastering the memory tricks and techniques in this book will be significantly easier if you are physically fit and have a positive outlook.

RELAX

While slight anxiety can help your memory, heavy stress can block it. If anxiety makes your mind go blank, daily use of relaxation techniques can help to create the calm mental state that is conducive to recalling stored information.

EASY ON DRUGS, ALCOHOL, AND SMOKING

Cutting down on drugs, drinking, and smoking can improve mental performance. Marijuana in particular has been found to impair memory function seriously. Consumer demand is growing, however, for the new "smart" drugs and nutrients that are believed to improve mental function, including memory. Many of these claim dramatic results, but none of them should be taken without medical advice.

PUT YOURSELF IN A STIMULATING ENVIRONMENT

During the mid-1980s, William T. Greenough of the University of Illinois performed a series of experiments to study the effect of stimulation on rats. One group of rats was kept in an empty, bare cage, while another lived in an environment filled with toys, wheels, and merry-go-rounds. The rats that inhabited the fun-filled cages developed 20 percent more brain synapses, or interconnections between nerves, than did the deprived rats, which indicated a considerable increase in brain activity. It is logical to infer that people benefit in a similar way from an environment in which they are stimulated and challenged.

KEEP FIT, EAT WELL

Exercise is essential for mental as well as physical fitness. When you are generally healthy, eating properly, and getting adequate exercise, your mind can process information more efficiently, and you are able to recall things easily and quickly. Studies have shown that a lack of physical exercise can slow down your memory response time.

REWARD YOURSELF

When you achieve a particular memory goal or perform an especially difficult task, reward yourself with a small indulgence or luxury. This will reinforce your accomplishment and encourage you to continue your efforts to encode information efficiently. Never underestimate the power of positive conditioning. Instead of saying, "My memory is so poor," try saying "I find my memory's getting better all the time."

LET SOME THINGS GO!

People tend to remember best what enhances their lives and makes them feel good, and to forget what isn't necessary, or what inspires dislike or fear. This selective forgetting is a perfectly healthy mechanism. General happiness can depend as much on the ability to forget some things as on the ability to remember.

If you need encouragement to keep up your memory regimen, remember this: The benefits of a better memory may be subtle, yet in the long run they are immeasurable. You may have an organized diary that lists all your engagements, but it won't help you if you leave it back at the office. Your memory, on the other hand, goes where you go. A better memory helps with personal details too. If your colleague told you that he would be away from the office to attend a funeral, it would save you and him embarrassment if you remembered this, and considered his feelings when you next saw him. A good memory could result in a promotion at work, allow you to spend less time reviewing for exams, or give you more confidence at parties.

Executive approval

In the business world, particularly, the rewards to be gained from having a good memory are tangible and monetary. Senior executives around the world in all areas of commerce and industry agree on one thing—the importance of memory is paramount. Memory keeps you in control of your business affairs and remembering well is the mark of a professional. To quote Arthur Levitt, Jr., former chairman of the American Stock Exchange: "To forget can be extraordinarily costly, not so much from a dollars-and-cents point of view as from a practical business point of view. [It] can also be extremely costly in terms of credibility."

So fight the habit of forgetting. As we have seen, a large part of memory problems derive from bad habits and laziness. Prepare yourself for success: Imagine sitting at the telephone without needing a phone book; or being able to supply a friend with a piece of information, confidently and accurately; or being able to enjoy meeting new people, knowing you will remember their names.

By reminding yourself of all the benefits of having an improved memory you are providing yourself with an essential ingredient: motivation. Whatever your memory goal, whether general or specific, with motivation you will be able to concentrate on the material you wish to learn and are thus more likely to remember it.

Keep using your memory, test it, and be creative with it. Push it to its limit. Surprise yourself with your abilities and newfound expertise.

REMEMBER TO DO IT!

If you often forget to do everyday things, there are a number of simple tricks that can help. One familiar tactic is to put a safety pin on the handle on your purse or briefcase; when it catches your eye, it will trigger your memory. Or wear your watch on the wrong wrist; when you look for your watch, your bare wrist will act as a reminder. A similar gimmick is to slip an elastic band around your wrist; you might associate your left hand with things connected with home and the right hand with work matters. While you might feel foolish with elastic bands on your wrists, this old trick can be extremely effective.

Making it obvious

Another way of jogging your memory is to alter the location or position of objects in a room. The next time you remember something you need to do just as you are nodding off to sleep, and don't want to get up and write a note, just tip your lampshade or put the alarm clock on the floor to set up a memory jogger for the morning. If you remember your next day's task before you are in bed, try leaving a dresser drawer wide open. Or stick a large note where it cannot be missed—on the refrigerator door, or by the front door, where you will be sure to notice it. Leaving your empty sports bag where you will trip over it in the morning would make sure you packed it and took it with you the next day. To remind yourself to do something before you leave the house, place a stone, nut, or a similar small object in the toe of your shoe, or tie the shoelaces together.

Remembering to do something regularly, but only for a limited period, is easier if you link it to a regular activity that has become truly automatic. If, say, you need to take a course of daily pills, place the container beside your toothbrush so it will catch your eye every morning when you brush your teeth.

KIM'S GAME

This memory exercise was adapted from a story by Rudyard Kipling published in 1901. In Kipling's tale, a poor street urchin named Kim is recruited to be a British spy in India. As part of his training, he is introduced to a game in which he must look for a second or two at a tray scattered with jewels and then remember each one in detail.

To play a similar game, look at the objects shown here for 30 seconds, then close the book and see how many you can remember. Do this before you read any further.

To recall these objects in so short a time, you will need to organize them into groups. You can sort them by similarities—eyeglasses, glass, and magnifying glass—or by the first letter of the object's name. An alternative is to tell a story about them: A woman wearing the pearl necklace and cupid brooch is rolling the dice in a casino.

Try playing the game with friends. Steadily increase the number of objects and cut the time. With practice you'll achieve startling results.

SOLUTIONS

Page 8:
True or false?
1. False. Your memory cannot become full. It can store an infinite amount of information.
2. False. Research has shown that although older people may have difficulty in paying attention, and hence in acquiring new information, they still retain an extensive store of general knowledge.
3. True. If you are not interested in something you are less likely to concentrate on it. Learning material in which you are not interested is also hard because you have less background knowledge to which you can relate new material.
4. False. In some cases anxiety seems to increase our ability to recall material, but fear has the opposite effect.
5. False. Your memory will improve with use.
6. False. People with amnesia cannot recall large amounts of information, but they can still remember many skills, such as how to read and write.
7. True. Physical exercise can increase the speed with which you learn and can improve your speed of recall.
8. True. A vitamin deficiency, drinking alcohol, and smoking can have a detrimental effect on your memory.
9. False. While memories rich in visual imagery are usually long lasting, a vivid memory can be inaccurate.
10. True. Younger people learn more quickly than older people. However, an older person's slowness to learn is often more related to a lack of enthusiasm than to decreased ability.
11. False. Although information that is learned is generally retained permanently, it can be lost through the destruction of brain tissue. The primary causes of this sort of brain damage are injury, disease, drugs, and alcohol abuse.
12. True. Memories become distorted by other memories, by your mood, and by the passing of time.

Page 32:
Memory for world events
1. The Austrian President Kurt Waldheim was refused entry to the U.S. following allegations of his involvement in Nazi atrocities during World War II.
2. Fred Astaire, who starred in films such as *Top Hat* (1935) and *Easter Parade* (1948). He died at age 88.
3. The American frigate *Stark* was hit by two Exocet missiles while patrolling the Persian Gulf. The missiles were fired by Iraqi Mirage jets.
4. British Prime Minister Margaret Thatcher. She was eventually forced to resign in November 1990.
5. *Sunflowers*, by Vincent van Gogh. The record stood for eight months before Van Gogh's *Irises* was sold at Sotheby's for £30 million.
6. Rudolph Hess, Adolf Hitler's former deputy, killed himself with an electric flex while in prison.

Pages 34 to 35:
Retrieval cues
You could have used any of the following headings to organize the objects: transport, tools, animals, food, flying things, yellow objects, or striped objects. The correct way to group them is the one that suits you. If you recalled fewer than 10 objects you have room to improve your memory. Your memory is average if you managed to recall between 11 and 15 objects. Recalling 16 to 20 objects indicates a good memory.

Pages 36 to 37:
Scripted scenes
Most people remember the sequence as an ordinary visit to a dentist's office by using a script that their memory already holds. If you remembered some unusual details, you probably made sense of them by adapting them to fit this script. For instance: The receptionist is holding some groceries for a client; a policemen has come in for a checkup; a photographer is taking shots for a feature on dentistry; and the receptionist has her coat on ready to leave. If you didn't refer to a dentist script, however, you might recall the sequence very differently. If, for example, you related your visit to a crime script, the policeman would be waiting to arrest the woman in the dentist's chair, but a local reporter in search of a scoop would have managed to snap her first.

Page 37:
Biased thinking

To understand any situation, you use your scripted knowledge. In the first picture shown below, the raised hand suggests physical violence, and a crying child is usually unhappy or in pain. Combining the two assumptions, you probably came to the conclusion that the parent is physically punishing the child. In reality the situation may have been different. The second picture below shows the same situation from a different viewpoint: Perhaps the child has been frightened by a wasp, and the parent is swatting it away from her head.

Page 43:
Filling in the gaps

Here are the incomplete and complete outlines of the four objects.

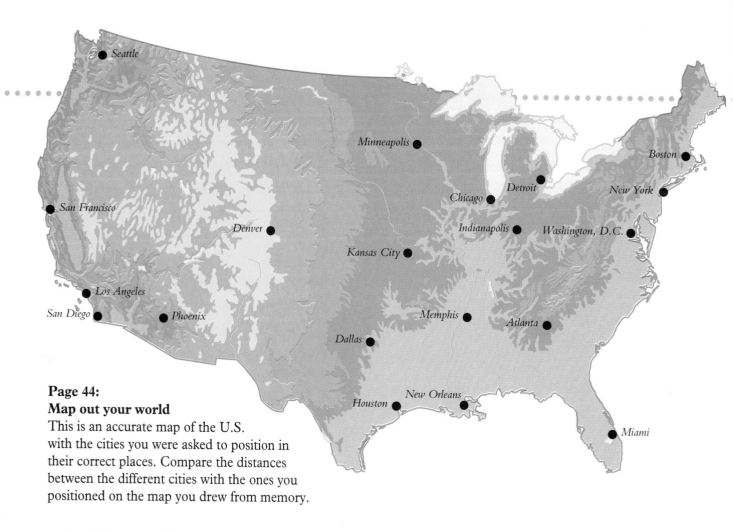

Page 44:
Map out your world
This is an accurate map of the U.S. with the cities you were asked to position in their correct places. Compare the distances between the different cities with the ones you positioned on the map you drew from memory.

Pages 44 and 47:
Spot the difference
There are 10 differences between the two illustrations. Compare the following: The mug in the man's hand, the woman's shoes, the right-hand curtain (which has moved), the lampshade, and the vase on the table in the foreground. There is no longer a cushion on the sofa, and the picture on the wall has changed. On the bookcase, the box and jug have swapped positions, and there is a new plant on the top shelf. Finally, the books on the second shelf of the bookcase are now lying on their sides instead of standing upright.

To spot all 10 differences in the pictures requires good observational skills and a strong visual memory of the first picture. A person with a good visual memory will score 8 or above on this test. If you noticed fewer than 5 differences, your visual memory is below average. A score of between 5 and 7 indicates an average recall.

Page 46:
Test your visual memory
Something was missing from each of these pictures. The version you saw on page 46 is shown in the left-hand column, and the correct version is shown in the right-hand column. The Coca-Cola logo was missing a hyphen, and Uncle Sam's hat was missing a star. A framed picture was dropped from the background of *Arrangement in Gray and Black* (Whistler's mother), and the Statue of Liberty's crown had too few spikes.

INCORRECT PICTURES

CORRECT PICTURES

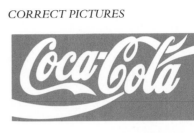

Page 55:
Remember yourself
The following political events happened during:
Reagan administration—Argentina invades the Falklands (April 1982).
Carter administration—Ayatollah Khomeini takes over in Iran (February 1979).
Reagan administration—Egyptian President Sadat is assassinated (October 1981).
Carter administration—Soviet Union invades Afghanistan (December 1979).
Carter administration—Margaret Thatcher becomes Prime Minister (May 1979).

These nonpolitical events happened during:
Carter administration—911 die in Jonestown suicides (November 1978).
Carter administration—Elvis Presley dies, aged 42 (August 1977).
Reagan administration—Jimmy Connors beats John McEnroe to win Wimbledon men's singles (July 1982).
Reagan administration—Pope John Paul wounded in Rome (May 1981).
Reagan administration—Prince Charles marries Lady Diana Spencer (July 1981).

Page 81:
Facial inversion
The inverted faces belong to Bill Cosby (left), Elizabeth Taylor (center), and John Lennon (right).

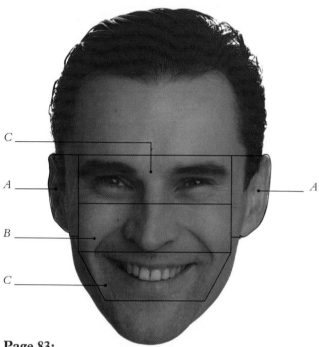

Page 83:
Test your memory for faces
The correct features that make up the face are: eyes **C**, nose **B**, mouth **C**, and ears **A**.

Page 91:
The name game
The correct answers (and suggested ways you might remember them) are:

1. **Ms. Kuzak:** Imagine her dancing round the room in a Russian cossack outfit.
2. **Mrs. Phillips:** She is wielding a Phillips screwdriver.
3. **Ms. Nanda:** She arrived on a panda.
4. **Mr. Mehmet:** He stammers, "We already me-met."
5. **Ms. Appleby:** Imagine her trying to balance an apple on her head while a bee is pestering her.
6. **Mr. Van der Meer:** Imagine him driving a van complaining, "Dear, dear!" at other drivers.
7. **Mr. O'Leary:** He says, "But I'm not at all dreary."
8. **Mr. Blitz:** He is in a shelter during an air raid.
9. **Ms. Dinard:** She eats a hard dinner—of stones.
10. **Mrs. Sorenson:** Think of her saying "Sorry, son."
11. **Ms. Larkins:** Picture her getting up with the lark.
12. **Mr. Sikorski:** Think of him flying a helicopter.

Page 114:
Distorted memories
Two groups of people were asked to recreate the line drawings on page 114 from memory. The first group was provided with the same captions as those on page 114. The second group was shown the same images but with different words (below, right-hand column). Here are examples of the drawings they produced.

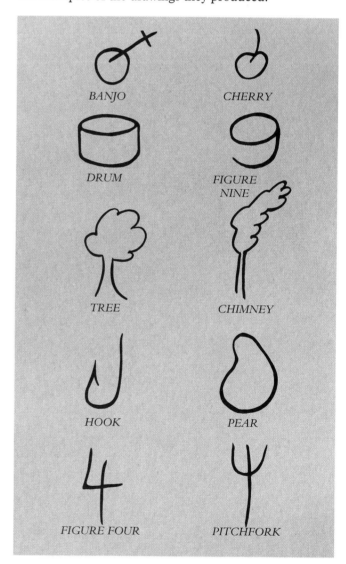

BANJO   *CHERRY*

DRUM   *FIGURE NINE*

TREE   *CHIMNEY*

HOOK   *PEAR*

FIGURE FOUR   *PITCHFORK*

Although each group of people were confident that they had remembered and redrawn the images as close to the originals as possible, in each case the real memory of the drawings was confused by the written descriptions provided. By comparing the two sets of drawings it is easy to see how much influence written material has over the visual memory of the objects.

Page 118:
A street crime
1. She was carrying a brown briefcase.
2. The pickpocket's victim was wearing a black jacket, white shirt, and grey trousers.
3. The woman with the bicycle saw the pickpocket.
4. The bicycle was white.
5. The woman in the orange jumper was carrying a plant.
6. The victim was concentrating on talking to the woman next to him.
7. Two women were having their photograph taken.
8. The man in the black leather jacket was taking a photograph.
9. None.
10. One person was wearing yellow.

If you scored 4 or less, your observation skills are poor. A score of 5 to 7 is average; 8 and above shows good observation skills.

A *B* *C* *D* *E*

Pages 118 and 119:
Identity parade
B is the pickpocket. In the original picture, the pickpocket was wearing a white T-shirt. For this reason, you may have chosen D. If you vaguely remember that there was a dark-haired man in the picture who was wearing a black leather jacket, you may have chosen E. Or you may have chosen the wrong man simply because you were guessing what he looked like.

Page 119:
Traffic accident
1. The color of the second car passing by the accident was black.
2. Yes, the traffic lights changed from red to green, but it was after the accident.
3. The colors of the cars involved were blue and red.
4. The driver of the blue car indicated his intention to turn left (not right) before the accident.

INDEX

Page numbers in *italics* refer to illustrations; page numbers in **bold** refer to memory exercises.

A

Acronyms, 63
Acrostics, 63-64
Actors' lines, 20
Advertisements, use of memory techniques in, 65, 67
Aging, effect on memory, 80, 108-109, 110
Astaire, Fred, 136
Aitken, Prof. A.C., 99
Alcohol abuse, 110-111
Alzheimer's disease, 110, 111
Ambiguity, perceptual, 43
American Gothic (Grant Wood), 77
Amnesia, 110, 111
  childhood, 106-108
  partial, 53
Anemia, 109
Arrangement in Gray and Black (J.M. Whistler), *46, 139*
Association, 60, 61-62, 77
  personal, 93-95
Attention, 19, 27, 29, 41
  names, 84-85
Awareness, spatial, 42-45

B

Bartlett, Sir Frederick, 38-39
Brain activity, *24-25*
Brayshaw, Reverend, 97-98
Bush, President George, 55,

C

California State University, 57
Camillo, Giulio, 75
Carter, President Jimmy, 55, 139
Challenger space shuttle disaster, 56
Chaplin, Charlie, 50
Charles, Prince, 55, 139
Chunking, 28, 92-95
City Lights (movie), 50
Claparède, Edouard, 111
Concentration, 19, 27, 29, 41
  on names, 84-85
Connors, Jimmy, 55, 139
Conran, John, 125

Context dependency, 48-50
  recreation of context, 51
Crocodile Dundee (movie), 32

D

Dean, John, 55
Depression, influence on memory, 109
Descriptions, verbal, 81
Digit span, **14**, 27, 28, 93
Distortions of memory, 112-117, **114**
Distributed practice (study technique), 104-105

E

Ebbinghaus, Hermann, 102-103, 105
Electroencephalography (EEG), 24
Emotions, influence on memory, 50-51, 53, 109, 128
Events, historical, **32**, 55-56, **55**, 98
Experiences, personal (episodic), 31, 52-56, **55**, 108-109
Eyewitnesses, **112-113**, 114-117, **114, 118-119**

F

Faces, remembering, 80-82, **83, 114, 116**
  inversion, **81**
  linking to names, 84-87, 90
Falklands war, 55, 139
Filling in the gaps (visual memory test), **43**
Forgetting, 101, 102-108, 110-111
  Ebbinghaus forgetting curve, 102-103
Freud, Sigmund, 90

G

Galton, Sir Francis, 52
"Galton's number" (personal memory), 52
Gender, relationship to memory, 46, 80
Geographical awareness
  local, **45**
  national, **44**
Greenough, William T., 132

H

Haley, Alex (*Roots: The Saga of an American Family*), 8
Health, 109, 132
Hess, Rudolph, 136
Hiding places, 69, 71, 105
History, 8, **32**, 55-56, **55**, 98
  names, 125-127
Hypermnesia, 108
Hypnosis, 57

I

Identity parade, **118-119**
Illness, influence on memory, 109
Images, visual *See* Visualization
Inaccuracies, 21, 112-117
Information storage, 13, 18-21, 30-33, **34**
Interference, 28, 104
  proactive, 106, 115
  retroactive, 105-106, 115
Interpreting what you see, **37**
Iran-Contra hearings, 32
Irises (V. van Gogh), 136

J

James, William, 102
John Paul II, Pope, 55, 139
Johnson, Samuel, 19
Jonestown suicides, 55, 139

K

Kennedy, President John F. (assassination), 56
Khomeini, Ayatollah, 55, 139
Kim's game, **134**
Knowledge, general (semantic), 31-33, **32**, 108-109
Korsakoff's syndrome, 110-111

L

Language, 31, 33, 68
  foreign, 61, 104-105, 106
Lawson, Prof. Alvin, 57
Learning, 60, 109, 128-129
Levitt, Arthur, Jr., 133
Loci system, 74-79
Locke, John, 48-49, 50
Loftus, Elizabeth, 114, 116

M

Magnetic resonance imaging (MRI), 24

Mahadevan, Rajan, 98
Maps, 44, 45-47
Mathematics, 98, 99
Memorabilia (memories inspired by objects), 52, 54
Memories
  childhood, 52-53, 106-108
  "flashbulb," 55-56
Memory
  episodic, 31, 52-56, **55**, 108-109
  long-term, 18, 19, 20, 21-23, 26, 29, 30-33, **34-35**
  photographic, 41
  procedural, 31, 33
  semantic, 331-33, **32**, 108-109
  sensory, 6, **17**, 18, 19, 20, 21-23, 27, 28, 50
    See also Senses
  short-term, **14-17**, 18, 19, 20, 21-23, 24, 26-29
  state-dependent, 50-51
  visual, 40-47, **43-47**
  working, 26-29
    See also Memory, short-term
Memory blocks, 90, 110-111
Memory exercises, **14-17,**
  biased thinking, **37**
  distorted memories, **114**
  faces, **81, 83, 114, 116**
  general evaluation, **9**
  geography, **44, 45**
  identity parade, **118-119**
  Kim's game, **134**
  name game, **88-89, 91**
  remembering your past, **54**
  retrieval cues, **34-35**
  scripted scenes, **36-37**
  spot the difference, **44, 47**
  story telling, **38-39**
  street crime, **112-113, 118**
  traffic accident, **115, 119**
  true or false?, **8**
  visual memory, **43-47**
  world events, **32, 55**
Memory techniques, 59, 121, 122-124
  association, 60, 61-62, 77, 93-95
  chunking, 28, 92-95
  fingers for multiplication, using, 99
  linking names and faces, 84-87
  method of the loci, 74-79

mnemonics, 60-65
numbers into letters, 96-97
numbers into pictures, 95-98
peg-word system, 72-73
repetition, 60-61
tips from waiters, 125
visualization, 60, 66-71, 74-79
word prompts, 54
Mental activity network scanner
(MANSCAN), *24-25*
Method of the loci, 6, 74-79,
126-127, 131
Misplaced memories, 33, 42
Mnemonics, 60-65
capital cities, 65
chemical elements, 73
colors of the rainbow, 64
days in each month, 62-63
Great Lakes, 63
Lincoln's assassination, 97
medical facts, 63-64, 124
musical notes, 64
packing for a vacation, 124-125
planets, 62-63
spelling, 60, 62, 63
word meanings, 61, 68
U.S. presidents, 125-127
Mona Lisa (Leonardo da Vinci),
40-41
Moods, influence on memory,
50-51, 53, 109, 132
influence on studying, 128
Motion pictures, 27
Motor skills (procedural memory),
31, 33

N

Names, remembering, **14-17**,
84-87, 90
blocks, 85, 90
game, **88-89**, **91**
historic, 125-127
links to faces, 84, 85, **88-89**, **91**
Nines times table, **99**
Nixon, President Richard, 55
Numbers, remembering, 10,
64-65, 92-99, 122-123
as dates, 98
Brayshaw's system, 97
chunking, 10, 92-95
digit span, **14**
numbers into letters, 96-97
numbers into pictures, 95-98

O

O'Brien, Dominic (memory
expert), 6
Organization of memories, 11, 29,
30-31, 62
relatedness, 32-33, **34-35**
time dating, 31, **32**, 55-56,
55

P

Peg-word system, 72-73, 74, 127,
131
Penfield, Wilder, 24
Places as reminders, 74-79
Planets, 62-63
Positron emission tomography
(PET), *25*
Practice, memory, 9, 60, 121,
130, 131
distributed, 104-105
faces, 87
hypermnesia, 108
loci system, 75-79, 126-127
names, 87
personal memories, 54, 56
visualization, 70-71
visual memories, 47
Presidents, U.S., remembering
names and chronological
order of, 97, 125-127
Presley, Elvis, 55, 139
Prosopagnosia, 80
Proust, Marcel *(Remembrance of
Things Past)*, 50
"Proustian memory," 50
Puns, 65, 73

Q

Questions, leading, 116-117

R

Reagan, President Ronald, 55,
139
Relatedness, 32-33, **34-35**
Remembering
addresses, *96*, 123
dates, 97
exam material, 128-129
faces, 80-82
languages, 61, 68
lists, 16-17, 34, 72-73, 75,
76-77, 78-79, 124-125
names, 31, 69, 84-90, 123

numbers, 10, 64-65, 92-99,
122-123
routes, 47
speeches, 124
spelling, 62, 63
to do things, 67, 68, 133
where you put things, 51, 69,
71, 105
your past, 48-51, 54, **54**, 56, 57,
106, 108,
Remembrance of Things Past (M.
Proust), 50
Reminders, **34-35**, 52, 54, 133
See also Safe places
Repetition, 60-61
Restak, Richard M., 6
Retrieval cues, **34-35**, 52,
54, 133
Rhymes, 62-63, 72, 73
*Roots: The Saga of an American
Family* (A. Haley), 8
Routes, 45-47, **45**

S

Sadat, President Anwar, 55, 139
Safe places, 69, 71, 105
See also Reminders
Schemas *See* Scripts
Scripts, 36-39, **36-37**, 38-39,
115
Senses
sight, 27, 40-47, **43-44**,
46-47, 115
smell, 20, 50, 115
sound, 20-21, 28, 50, 115
Serial position phenomenon, 17
Shakespeare, William, 20
Shereshevskii, S.V. (memory
expert), 6, 6-8, 75, 101
Simonides (Greek poet), 74
Space, three-dimensional,
42-45
Spaceships, alien, 57
Speech making, 124
Spelling, 62, 63
Spencer, Lady Diana, 55, 139
Spot the difference, **44**, **47**
Storage of information
See Organization
Stories from ancestors, 8
Street crime, (observation test),
112-113, **118**
Studying techniques, 128-129

Sunflowers (V. van Gogh), 136
Surgery patients, 111
Synesthesia, 6, 50

T

Telephone numbers,
remembering, 64, 65, 96, 97
Test your memory, **14-17**
Test your visual memory, **46**
Time, effect of, 102, 115-116
Time dating (episodic memories),
31, **32**, 55-56, **55**, 98
Tip-of-the-eye phenomenon
(TOE), 107
Tip-of-the-tongue phenomenon
(TOT), 107
Traffic accidents, **115**, **119**
True or false? (quiz), **8**

U

University of Illinois, 132

V

Van Gogh, Vincent, 136
Vacation preparation, 124-125
Violence, effect on eyewitness
memory, 117
Visualization, 60, 66-71
loci system, 74-79
peg-word system, 72-73
safe places, 69, 71, 105
tips from waiters, 125
Von Restorff effect (memory
phenomenon), 17

W

Waldheim, President Kurt, 136
Wall Street crash, 32
War of the Ghosts (Sir F. Bartlett),
38-39
Watergate hearings, 55
Whistler, James McNeill
*(Arrangement in Gray and
Black)*, 46, 139
Wood, Grant *(American Gothic)*,
77
Words, as prompts, **34-35**, 54
World events, 31, **32**, 55-56,
55, 98

Z

Zodiac signs, used as
mnemonics, 77

BIBLIOGRAPHY

Alan Baddeley, *Human Memory: Theory and Practice*; Lawrence Erlbaum Associates, Hillsdale, NJ, U.S., 1991

Alan Baddeley, *Your Memory: A User's Guide*; Macmillan Publishing Company, New York, NY, U.S., 1982

Ludy T. Benjamin, Jr., J. Roy Hopkins and Jack R. Nation, *Psychology*; Macmillan Publishing Company, Inc., New York, NY, U.S., 1987

William Buskist and David W. Gerbin, *Psychology: Boundaries and Frontiers*; Scott, Foresman/Little, Brown Higher Education, Glenview, IL, U.S., 1990

Tony Buzan, *Make the Most of Your Mind*; Pan Books, London, U.K., 1988

Tony Buzan, *Use Your Memory*; BBC Books, London, U.K., 1989

Gillan Cohen, *Memory in the Real World*; Lawrence Erlbaum Associates, Hillsdale, NJ, U.S., 1991

Ward Dean and John Morgenthaler, *Smart Drugs and Nutrients*; B & J Publications, Santa Cruz, CA, U.S., 1991

Karen G. Duffy, *Annual Editions: Psychology 1992/1993*; Duskin Publishing Group, Inc., Guilford, CT, U.S., 1992

Bruno Furst, *Stop Forgetting*; Doubleday and Company, Inc., Garden City, NY, U.S., 1972

John R. Hayes, *The Complete Problem Solver*; Lawrence Erlbaum Associates, Hillsdale, NJ, U.S., 1989

Douglass J. Hermann, *Super Memory*; Wing Books, New York, NY, U.S., 1991

Patricia S. Goldman-Rakic, "Working Memory and the Mind," *Scientific American*; September 1992, pages 110-117

Richard L. Gregory, ed., *The Oxford Companion to the Mind*; Oxford University Press, Oxford, U.K., 1989

Kenneth A. Klivington, *The Science of Mind*; The MIT Press, Cambridge, MA, U.S., 1989

Harry Lorayne, *Memory Makes Money: How to Get Rich Using the Power of Your Mind*; Thorsons Publishing Group, Wellingborough, U.K., 1988

Joan Minninger, *Total Recall: Successfully Boost Your Memory Power*; Thorsons Publishing Group, Wellingborough, U.K., 1987

Rod Plotnik, *Introduction to Psychology*; Random House, New York, NY, U.S., 1989

Spencer A. Rathus, *Psychology*; Holt, Rinehart and Winston, Inc., Orlando, FL, U.S., 1987

Richard M. Restak, "Memories are made of this," *1992 Yearbook of Science and the Future*; Encyclopedia Britannica, Inc., Chicago, Il, U.S., 1992

Richard M. Restak, *The Mind*; Bantam Books, New York, NY, U.S., 1988

Peter Russell, *The Brain Book*; Routledge, London, U.K., 1990

Oliver Sacks, *The Man Who Mistook His Wife for a Hat*; Pan Books, London, U.K., 1985

Robert L. Solso, *Cognitive Psychology*; Allyn and Bacon, Inc, Boston, MA, U.S., 1988

"*Your memory is better than you think.*"

Douglas J. Herrmann

"*God gave us our memories so that we might have roses in December.*"

James M. Barrie